Kake –Jiku

IMAGES OF JAPAN IN APPLIQUÉ, FABRIC ORIGAMI, AND SASHIKO

Kumiko Sudo

Breckling Press

Library of Congress Cataloging-in-Publication Data
Sudo, Kumiko.
   Kake-jiku : images of Japan in applique, fabric origami, and sashiko /
Kumiko Sudo.
     p. cm.
   ISBN 1-933308-11-7 (pbk.)
   1. Textile crafts—Japan. 2. Appliqué—Japan—Patterns. 3.
Quilting—Japan—Patterns. I. Title.

   T T699.S832 2006
   746.0952—dc22

                                          2006026395

Editorial direction by Anne Knudsen
Cover and interior design by Kim Bartko
Cover and interior photographs by Sharon Hoogstraten
Calligraphy and water color paintings by Kumiko Sudo
Technical drawings by Katherine Wager Wright

My heartfelt thanks to friends and students in Japan who have
generously shared their kimono fabrics. Thanks also to Yuwa Fabrics
and Clover Needlecraft, Inc.

Published by Breckling Press
283 N. Michigan Ave., Elmhurst, IL 60126

Printed and bound in China
International Standard Book Number: 1-933308-11-7

Contents

月よかぜ
ゆかせて
おくり
かの国の
水のことば
光の
はなし

Wind, oh, wind. Please tell me what you know.

Tell me the words of blue waters and

the stories that shimmering lights tell you.

Dear Readers

読者の皆様へ

IF YOU ARE FAMILIAR WITH my earlier books, you know that the inspirations for my designs often come from memories of my early life in Japan. Over time, the beautiful and heartwarming experiences of childhood and of the people and places I knew when I was young have harmonized into a melody that has stayed in my heart. The world around me today plays its part, too, in the quilts I make. Novel line movements, warm combinations of circles or other shapes, and special arrays of color can make me feel like dancing.

There is nothing I enjoy more than playing with my design ideas and developing them into quilts or other fabric art. Each book I write, from concept to finished projects, can engage me for as long as two years. Of course, during that time, I also work on other new ideas. While my hands keep stitching current creations, my thoughts fly ahead to future projects. As I listen to music, browse through my collection of art books, or watch movies, I collect new images and they are all absorbed into my work. In the art world, creations by geniuses like Gustave Klimt, Wassily Kandinsky, and Aubrey Beardsley never fail to inspire me. Chatting with old friends on the phone, working in my garden, playing with my dogs—all these aspects of my daily life influence my designs and help me elaborate on them.

Sometimes I spend days choosing fabrics for a new project, though most of the time I make the decision in a flash of inspiration. I devote a lot of time, however, to *collecting* fabrics. I am particularly interested in combining Japanese kimono silks with contemporary cotton prints—I always enjoy the unpredictable beauty they produce in my work. As for fabric textures, I use various materials freely, from heavy drapery fabrics to light-weight gauzes. Looking for notions like decorative cords and trims is, for me, an exciting adventure. If I happen to find uniquely shaped objects at a flea market, for instance, I spend the rest of the day feeling as if I am floating on the clouds.

A few years ago I made a decision to give up teaching classes and workshops that involved travel. While I valued the time spent with students, I realized I was not able to successfully wear two hats at the same time. I chose a lifestyle that best suits my personality, staying close to home and committing myself to creating projects that I am can share through my books. By devoting my time to publishing my work, I believe I am able to produce ideas that will please and inspire those who enjoy my quilts.

Each new book is my way of thanking you, my readers, from the bottom of my heart for your support of my work. It is my dearest wish that you will continue to enjoy my creations through *Kake-Jiku* and future books that I write for you.

Kumiko Sudo

Creating Kake-Jiku

TSUKURIKATA NO ANNAI

A Guide to Technique

The projects in this book are inspired by traditional *kake-jiku*, the beautiful hanging scrolls found in most Japanese homes. A *kake-jiku* is a long strip of handmade Japanese paper and silk onto which a work of calligraphy or a piece of artwork is mounted or painted. Typically measuring 24″ wide by 60″ long, *kake-jiku* hang vertically on the wall, usually in an alcove. They are rolled up and put safely away when not in use. Many Japanese families change the *kake-jiku* on display with each season of the year. In doing so, we celebrate the coming of spring, summer, fall, or winter.

Kake-jiku are believed to have derived from Buddhist scrolls brought to Japan from China in the eleventh century. Their purpose was to aid in the teaching of Zen Buddhism. Early Buddhist scrolls displayed mounted sutras, inspired by teachings from Buddhist scriptures or images of Buddhist deities. These scrolls were hung on the walls of rooms where Buddhist monks conducted spiritual training. It was the practice of monks to place offerings of flowers and votive paper lanterns at the base of the scrolls. People believed such arrangements to be sacred, part of a ritual of purification.

As time passed, the subjects depicted on hanging scrolls changed. Within the various schools of the Japanese tea ceremony (known collectively as *sado*), the subjects presented shifted from Buddhist-inspired figures to motifs that were familiar and easy to understand for ordinary Japanese people. A scroll might display a few lines of Chinese poetry, a *sumi-e* ink drawing of scenery, flowers, birds, or animals, or a verse from a traditional Japanese *haiku* poem. The popularity of motifs such as these led to the rise of celebrated *kake-jiku* artists. Many of their fine scrolls have survived to this day and are greatly valued as examples of Japanese art. My teacher of *kamakura-bori*, or traditional Japanese wood-carving, has a *kake-jiku* depicting the brave figure of Yoritomo Minamoto, the first Shogun of the Kamakura era. A friend who is a master of calligraphy displays scrolls illustrated with Chinese poetry or *sumi-e* ink drawings of Buddhist figures or beautiful snow scenes. Everybody is proud of their own *kake-jiku*.

Connoisseurs of *kake-jiku* choose their scrolls with great care. For example, in preparing for a tea ceremony, the host carefully selects a scroll with a theme that is appropriate to the season, the occasion, and the guests. It is a sign of respect at the beginning of the ceremony for participants to comment on the *kake-jiku* displayed, praising its beauty.

In Japanese homes, a *kake-jiku* is usually hung in the family *tokonoma*, a small raised alcove with a *tatami* mat floor. The alcove might also house a small chest of drawers where family valuables are kept. There might be a flower arrangement to symbolize the season or a particular ceremonial occasion, such as New Year's Day. The *tokonoma* is revered as a precious and holy place in the home, probably because of the Buddhist origination of *kake-jiku*. So strong is its religious association, that I remember being scolded by my mother for accidentally stepping into the *tokonomo* when my little friends came to play.

Whenever I see *kake-jiku*, I am deeply thankful that the traditional Japanese sense of beauty is alive in this and other art forms that are unique to Japan. No matter how our daily lives change, *kake-jiku* help us preserve our heritage and our artistic aesthetic.

Wall Quilts Inspired by Kake-Jiku

In *Kake-Jiku* you will find fifteen designs reminiscent of Japanese hanging scrolls. Each one is a tiny window into my memories of life in Japan. I am particularly fond of images that reflect the changing of the seasons as winter gives way to spring and summer fades into fall.

All of the designs in *Kake-Jiku* are created using appliqué. Some also feature fabric origami, where two pieces of fabric are sewn together then folded into shapes of beautiful three-dimensional flowers. Other designs use *sashiko*, a Japanese version of the quilting stitch. The stitching serves to highlight portions of the appliqué design, adding a little extra grace.

You may wish to follow the Japanese tradition of *kake-jiku* by making one or more designs each for spring, summer, fall, and winter. Choose colors and fabrics that are in tune with the pleasures of the season. When your first block is completed, find a special corner in your home to display it. On a low table below it, place an arrangement of fresh seasonal flowers. Keep an incense burner nearby, if you wish, and fill your home with the scents of the season. You will soon discover what fun it is to rearrange the display with each changing season.

Selecting Fabrics

Before you begin to work with fabrics, look for inspiration in the world around you. Whether you find blossoms on your own garden path, deep in the woods, or in exotic floral arrangements in a flower shop window, each can be recreated in fabric. Look carefully at the colors. A single flower offers an incredible range of hues. Look, too, at the forms of the petals, the buds, and the leaves.

The designs in *Kake-Jiku* are made from a mixture of contemporary American and Japanese cottons and silks. Some blocks feature exquisite Japanese silks, even some antique kimono fabrics. I am fortunate that friends and students in Japan send kimono fabrics that I am able to incorporate into my work. Today, Japanese motifs are popular in fabrics from a range of manufacturers as well as specialty distributors. A quick search of web sites that offer Japan-inspired fabrics will

get you started, as will a visit to the fabric stores in your area. Look for beautiful motifs that represent the seasons, such as flowers or trees, mountains or clouds. If you find motifs you love, it is easy to make the appliqué templates slightly larger or smaller than mine so that you can beautifully accommodate the images in those fabrics. While you may need to purchase fabric for the block base, the borders, and the backing, most of the appliqué designs can be made from scraps left over from other projects. Using the photographs of my designs as a guide to color contrast (the use of light, medium, and dark tones), I suggest you choose colors and patterns that you enjoy. Lay them out on the background fabric you have selected. Make sure, too, that the fabric you have chosen for the border complements the appliqué designs and does not overwhelm them.

Using Templates

For each project in *Kake-Jiku*, full-size templates are provided for all appliqués other than easy-to-draw squares, rectangles, and circles. The templates do not include seam allowances. Sometimes, you will need to draw around the templates to mark a design on your background fabric. When you are ready to cut out your fabric pieces, however, you will need to add a ⅛" or ¼" seam allowance to all appliqué templates. (The recommended seam allowance is indicated on the template.) Most of the templates are curved, which means they are easier to cut with very sharp scissors than with rotary cutting equipment. Since the projects are small and multiples of the same pattern piece are rarely needed, hand-cutting is quick and easy. Remember to transfer any markings from the pattern onto the cut pieces of fabric.

Sewing

I sew everything—straight seams and curved seams, piecing and appliqué—by hand. I like the sense of intimacy that hand-sewing gives me. I feel that the hand is directed not only by the eye but by the heart. Since all the dimensional flower designs are small, you may want to sew them by hand, too. You'll find

Basic Tool Kit

A list of materials is supplied with every project. In addition, you will need the items listed here. Collect everything you need before you start and keep it all in a box or basket within easy reach. A little preparation will save you time and frustration when you sit down to sew.

- Hand-sewing needles
- Pins and pincushion
- High-quality sewing or quilting needles (choose the smallest size you are comfortable with)
- Embroidery needle (large-eye) and/or *sashiko* needle
- High-quality hand-sewing threads in variety of colors
- *Sashiko* thread or 2-ply embroidery floss in a variety of colors
- Thimble
- Thread snips
- Self-healing cutting mat
- Rotary cutter (optional)
- Sharp fabric scissors
- Paper scissors
- Tailor's chalk, charcoal stick, or other temporary marker
- Sharp pencils and eraser
- Compass
- Ruler
- Tracing paper
- Template plastic or stiff card
- Toothpick or dollmaker's awl

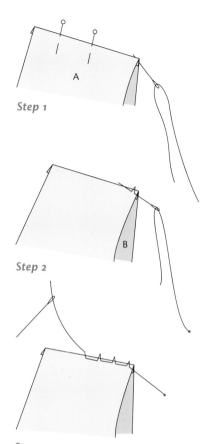

Step 1

Step 2

Step 3

that some require only a few stitches. If, however, you prefer to sew by machine, you will find it easy to do so. The circles and squares of back-to-back fabric from which most of the flowers are formed are simple to sew by machine. Adding the appliqués is also easy on the machine, as is adding the backing and borders.

Many of the designs involve sewing curved seams. For perfect curved seams, I use a form of appliqué or invisible stitching that is described below. My technique involves placing a fabric piece, with the seam allowance folded under, on top of a background piece; the piece is then blind-stitched by hand. In the instructions, this is what is meant by the term *appliqué*. The term *sew* indicates a more traditional method of sewing the pieces together, right sides facing, using a running stitch on the wrong side of the seam lines. Straight seams are sewn in this way, and you may use hand or machine stitching.

Appliqué Stitches

The appliqué technique I use to attach appliqués of flowers, leaves, and stems onto the background fabric results in tiny stitches that are not visible from the front of the quilt. The appliqués lie flat, for a smooth, clean effect.

1. Fold under the seam allowance of the appliqué and press or finger-press it firmly. Pin the appliqué in place through the seam allowance onto the background fabric. Knot the thread, then insert the needle at an angle through the fold line on the appliqué fabric (A). This will neatly hide the knot in the folded seam allowance.

2. Insert the needle through a single thread in the weave of background fabric (B). As soon as it emerges from fabric B, re-insert the needle into fabric A at the fold line. Exit at a point ¼" further along the fold line.

3. Repeat, pulling the thread firmly with each stitch. In effect, the thread is hidden in the "tunnel" inside the folded seam allowance of fabric A.

If you are working with slippery fabrics like silks or with small appliqués, it is helpful to baste the seam allowance of the appliqué firmly in place before beginning the appliqué stitch. This will prevent distortion of the fabric. Take care to fold over any tips or sharp corners precisely before basting. Remove the basting stitches once the appliqué is in place.

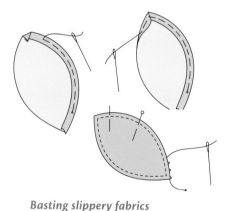

Basting slippery fabrics

Fabric Origami

The dimensional flower designs in *Kake-Jiku* are inspired by the Japanese art of origami, or paper folding. Like many Japanese children, I learned the basics of origami at my mother's knee. I loved the colors and patterns in decorative origami papers and would mold them into shapes of my own. Now, instead of paper, I fold fabrics. One difference between folding paper and folding fabric is that paper is available with different colors on the two sides. To achieve the same effect when folding fabric, you must first sew the two colors of your choice together, then turn them right side out and press.

Preparing Flower Shapes

All the origami flower designs begin with a simple shape—a circle, a square, or a pentagon. Use the same steps to prepare all shapes, as follows. All flower templates already include a ¼" seam allowance.

1. Using the templates indicated in the pattern you have selected, cut the fabrics as needed and arrange the shapes into pairs. Take care to achieve good color contrast between the fabrics in each pair.

2. Matching contrasting colors (light to dark) and right sides together, sew the pairs together by hand or by machine around the outer edges, leaving a 2" opening.

3. Fold the seams inward toward the center of the shape and press. If you are preparing a circle, follow the curved line to make a nice, rounded curve. For angled shapes, poke a toothpick or dollmaker's awl into the angles to assure crisp corners. Turn the shape right side out, then blind-stitch the opening closed. Lightly press to reinforce the shape.

Just as in traditional paper origami, which uses paper decorated in different colors and patterns on either side, you now have a two-sided shape to begin folding your flowers.

Even if you know nothing of origami, you will find that my fabric-folding techniques are easy to learn. These tips may help.

- Study each folding diagram carefully before you begin. Determine which is the right and wrong side of the fabric. You may find it helpful to practice each new shape on a sample so that you solve any difficulties before you begin on your final piece.
- Always fold accurately and neatly.
- Crease each fold firmly with the back of your thumbnail. Good creases make the folding easier, and they serve as guides to future steps.

You will find that the same procedures are used over and over again. You will soon become so proficient with them that you can carry them out almost without thinking.

Preparing the Background Base

All of the blocks in *Kake-Jiku* are the same size and are constructed in exactly the same way. The complete size, including borders, is 19″ × 19″. The border width is 2″. To prepare the background base onto which you will appliqué the design, follow these simple steps.

1. Cut a square of background fabric measuring 16″ × 16″. This includes ½″ seam allowance. The square may be cut from a single length of fabric or it may be pieced from two or more fabrics.

2. Mark a seam line ½″ inwards from all edges, so that background base onto which you will appliqué measures 15″ × 15″.

3. Carefully and lightly draw the complete design onto to background base, using the photograph and the layout diagram as guides. To begin, make a photocopy of all templates, preferably onto stiff card. Without adding seam allowances, cut out each shape. Position the shapes on the background base, then draw around each one. Transfer any *sashiko* designs onto the background base also.

4. Center the background base on top of the batting and baste the batting in place. Very thin batting works best and is easier to needle.

You are now ready to appliqué the design of your choice onto the background base.

Sashiko *Designs*

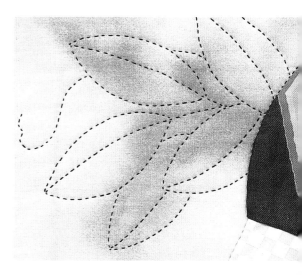

Rather than use the traditional quilting stitch, I have adapted Japanese *sashiko* stitching to embellish the blocks in *Kake-Jiku*. This delicate yet distinctive form of stitching accents the appliqué designs beautifully. The stitching might suggest rays of sunshine, a sudden breeze, or the fluttering wings of a butterfly. Your choice of a contrasting thread color may highlight such effects.

The method of stitching I have used is a combination of the traditional *sashiko* stitch and the quilting stitch. It is done before the backing and border are completed, so that the stitches do not show through to the back of the quilt. I use a selection of colorful sashiko threads or two-ply embroidery floss and a large-eye embroidery needle with a fine, sharp point. I like the quality of needles produced by Clover Needlecraft. DMC produces wonderful embroidery floss in a range of colors. I use DMC's #25 floss. (Floss is typically sold as six-ply, so you will need to cut a 12″ to 15″ length of thread then separate the strands before you begin stitching.)

1. Using the stencils provided with each pattern or drawing freehand, lightly mark the sashiko design on the background base. If your fabric is light and thin, you may be able to trace directly onto it using a light box. (If you do not have a light-box, tape the pattern to a sunlit window, then tape the fabric over it.)

2. Without knotting the thread, insert the needle from the front of the quilt, at a point about ¼″ away from first marked line of *sashiko*. Come up on the marked line, about ⅛″ beyond your starting point. Make a backstitch, inserting the needle at the marked starting point to secure the thread, then let the tail of the thread slip through to the back of the work. Use simple stab stitches to complete the design. For each stitch, pull the thread through all layers of the quilt, exiting on the back. Reinsert the needle from the back to the front, taking care to stay on the marked design.

3. Follow the stitching sequence provided with the *sashiko* pattern to complete the design. (For simple lines and circles, no stitching sequence is provided.) To finish stitching, make another backstitch, then pull the needle about ¼″ from this point. Clip the thread as close to the quilt as possible.

Stem stitch

Stem-Stitch Embroidery

Adding embroidery is a simple and elegant way to add subtle highlights to your sewing projects. For the projects in *Kake-Jiku*, there is no need to master a variety of stitches. With a minimum of practice, you can easily learn a basic stem stitch, which is all I use for these projects. The pretty vines in *Reading under the Vines* on page 92 add a light and delicate touch, complementing the appliqué designs.

Embroidery floss is available in an amazing range of colors and usually comes in six-ply packages. Cut a length of thread (if you work with 12″ lengths your work should remain tangle-free). Split off a double ply, then thread a large-eye embroidery needle. It is easy to work stem-stitch freehand. If you need a guideline, mark the pattern with a quilter's pencil or tailor's chalk.

Stem stitch is simply a line of staggered backstitches, each about ⅛″ long or less. Hide the knot on the underside of the fabric. Draw the thread through the fabric and re-enter about ⅛″ or the desired stitch length along your marked pattern. Turn the needle and come up again about half-way along and closely next to the first stitch. Take another stitch, progressing about ⅛″ along your pattern. Repeat and continue to the end.

Adding Backing and Borders

The first step in making each of the small quilts in *Kake-Jiku* is to prepare the background base onto which you will then appliqué the designs (see page 10). Unlike traditional quiltmaking, I always baste a layer of thin batting to the background base before I begin the appliqués. Once the design is complete, I add backing and borders. Each finished quilt measures 19″ × 19″ which includes a 2″ border. For the borders, I am always careful to choose a beautiful fabric that complements but does not overwhelm the appliqués.

Follow these steps to add the backing and border to the quilt top.

1. Pre-cut background base, batting, and backing/border fabric as shown here, or as directed in the pattern.

2. Baste the batting to the background base and complete the appliqués and *sashiko* designs as directed in the quilt pattern.

3. When the quilt design is complete, pin the quilt top (including the batting), wrong sides together, to the backing fabric. Make sure that the front and back align perfectly, with the batting extending by 2″ on all sides.

4. Fold inwards ½″ seam allowances along both long edges of each border piece. Press. Fold each border piece in half lengthwise and press.

5. Position and pin the top border in place, keeping the edge of the batting snug against the inside fold and aligning the folded edge at the front with the guideline marked around the outside of the background base (½″ inwards from the edge; see step 2 on page 10). Blind-stitch the border in place at the front and back. Repeat for the bottom border.

6. Fold inwards ½″ seam allowance at both short ends of each vertical border piece. Press. Repeat step 5 to sew the vertical borders in place. Blind-stitch the front border to the back border at the top and bottom.

MATERIALS FOR
BACKGROUNDS AND BORDERS

Background base: 16″ × 16″

Backing: 16″ × 16″

Batting: 19″ × 19″

Side borders, cut 2: 5″ × 20″

Top/bottom borders, cut 2: 5″ × 16″

A friend visited me and
we shared experiences and
emotions. How fast pleasant
time flies! The moon was
already high up in the
twilight sky.

誰かしら
たづねきたりて
わかちあい
楽しき時の
みじかし
夕月

Winter

FUYU

At the beginning of new year celebrations, my mother would always place a delicately crafted arrangement of pine branches and nandin berries in our tokonoma, a special raised alcove that is unique to Japanese homes. Behind it would hang one of her favorite kake-jiku, representing a New Year's theme. On New Year's Day, we would all gather around the tokonoma and pray for the health and happiness of the family. Many Japanese families enjoy the same tradition today.

In earlier times, a Japanese lady's comb meant as much to her as jewelry means to western women today. Decorative hair ornaments were an important fashion accessory. My mother often spoke of her delight when fancy goods vendors would call at her home, carrying boxes filled with row upon beautiful row of combs.

As a child, I always remember the hustle and bustle in the streets at year's end, as everyone ran last-minute errands in time for New Year. On a corner of the busy streets in my neighborhood, there was a store that sold old-fashioned Japanese wigs, of the type usually worn with traditional kimono. In the window displays, the wigs were often adorned with elegant ornamental combs. Made from high-quality boxwood, they were intricately hand carved and hand-decorated. Some were so pretty they are vivid in my memory today. I can still see a special comb decorated with tiny flowers that were made by folding pink, white, yellow, and green silks into petals and leaves. Pressing my face to the glass pane of the show window, I remember gazing at that comb, thinking, "Oh, I want one . . ."

Combs KUSHI 櫛

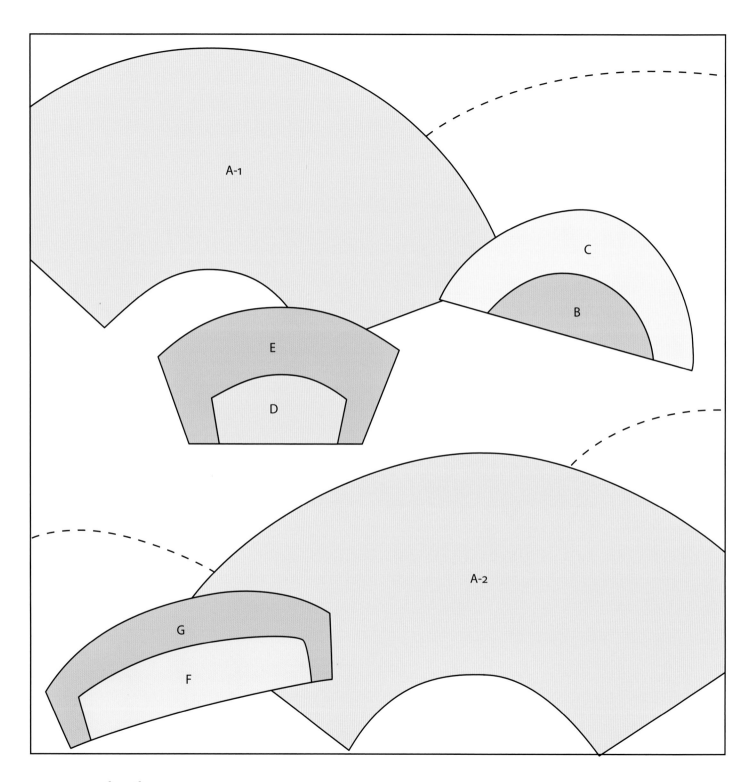

YOU WILL NEED

Background base: 16″ × 16″

Backing : 16″ × 16″

Batting: 19″ × 19″

Side borders, cut 2: 5″ × 20″

Top/bottom borders, cut 2: 5″ × 16″

Comb shapes: Large scraps of one fabric;
   small scraps of six more fabrics

Sashiko thread or 2-ply embroidery floss

_____

Use templates on pages 111–112, adding seam allowances indicated.

Prepare base

1. Prepare the background base following the steps on page 10 and using the layout diagram as a guide.

2. Select fabrics for the appliqués. Add seam allowances to the templates. Cut out and prepare all appliqué pieces (A to G) by folding under the seam allowances, then pressing and pinning each in place onto the background base. You may need to snip the curves to make sure all pieces lie perfectly flat when pressed. Note that the large comb-shaped pieces A require a ¼″ seam allowance, while all others require just ⅛″.

3. Appliqué large comb shapes A in place. Appliqué the bottom edges of small comb pieces B, D, and F. Appliqué C, E, and G over their corresponding pieces, hiding the remaining raw edges of B, D, and F.

Sashiko

4. Create gently curved lines of stitching as in the layout diagram, imitating the curves of the larger combs. If necessary, use the curved edge of template A to mark the curve onto the background base before stitching. (See also page 11).

Complete

5. See page 13 for directions on adding the backing and borders.

Hanetsuki was a badminton-like game, usually played by girls at the beginning of the year. While the game itself is no longer popular, elaborately decorated *hagoita*—wooden raquets or battledores with which it was played—are still loved and collected as seasonal home decorations. Ornamental *hagoita*, richly embellished with gold and silver, were used long ago in the Imperial court during Japan's Edo period. Today, *hagoita* are made from lightweight paulownia board, and one side might be pasted with silk or handmade paper imprinted with the image of a celebrated kabuki actor or movie star.

Battledore

HAGOITA

羽子板

   As a child, I knew that the end of the year was drawing close when *hagoita* vendors set up their stalls on the grounds of temples or shrines. The sight of their colorful displays—often rising six feet high on wooden frames—reminded everyone that the new year was approaching. Most colorful of all were the *hane* or shuttlecocks, their feathers dyed in pink, red, violet, yellow and green. Rows and rows of them lined the pathways through the shrines.

   As year-end came near, we children would sing "How many nights will we sleep before the New Year arrives?" When the longed-for day finally dawned, I would play *hanetsuki* with my friends, trying my best not to miss the shuttlecock. Picture the scene on New Years Day: dozens of girls playing *hanatsuki*, sending brightly colored *hane* up into the crisp winter sky and watching as they whirled to the ground. I remember it as a beautiful rainbow in the winter sky.

YOU WILL NEED

Background base: 16″ × 16″

Backing : 16″ × 16″

Batting: 19″ × 19″

Side borders, cut 2: 5″ × 20″

Top/bottom borders, cut 2: 5″ × 16″

Battledores: Large scraps of three different fabrics

Handles: Fabric scraps

Shuttlecocks: Variety of scraps

Use templates on page 113, adding seam allowances indicated.

Prepare base

1. Prepare the background base following the steps on page 10 and using the layout diagram as a guide.

2. Select fabrics for the appliqués. Add seam allowances to the templates. Cut out and prepare all appliqué pieces (A to C) by folding under the seam allowances, then pressing and pinning each in place onto the background base. Note that the large battledore pieces A require a 1/4″ seam allowance, while all others require just ⅛″. Appliqué handle B, then battledores A-1 and A-2. Next, appliqué handle C and battledore A-3, overlapping the previous appliqués as indicated.

Make two shuttlecocks

3. Using template D, cut 20 from multicolored fabrics. Matching contrasting colors and right sides together, sew pairs together around the long edges as shown.

4. Turn right side out. Make five for each shuttlecock. Layer as shown, then sew the pieces together.

5. Using template E, cut two. Fold under the seam allowance and press in place. Appliqué to the background base, trapping the raw edges of the D units in place. If desired, add a few stitches to the outermost D units to attach the shuttlecocks securely to the background base.

Complete

6. See page 13 for directions on adding the backing and borders.

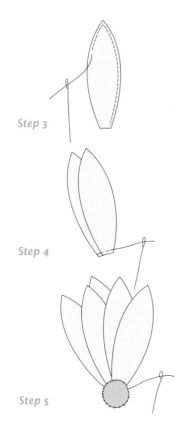

Step 3

Step 4

Step 5

Karuta are Japanese playing cards. The name comes from the Portuguese word *carta*, and the game played in Japan has its origins in a card game from Portugal. Long prior to the Portuguese influence, Heian-era courtiers would play a matching game with clamshells, known as *kai-uta*. A stack of shells was divided in two. The first part of a *waku* poem (a 31-syllable poem unique to Japan) would be written inside each shell in the first stack; the remainder of each poem would be written in the shells in the second stack. Once all the shells were filled with poems, the stacks were shuffled. When the first clamshell was presented, the players would try to find the matching shell to complete the poem. Clamshells were often exquisitely painted with themes from *waku* poetry, their rims embellished with gold. Particularly beautiful *kai-uta* sets were prized as works of art.

Portuguese missionaries brought cardboard playing cards to Japan about 400 years ago. Since then, *karuta* have gone through many changes, but the beautiful tradition of hand-painted clamshells has still left its traces in uniquely Japanese cards that are wonderfully illustrated, or feature Chinese kanji characters, poetry, or verses. When I was small, every family had *karuta*, often decorated with pictures or famous sayings. When we gathered to celebrate the beginning of a new year, children played *karuta* together while enjoying special sweets made only for New Year's Day.

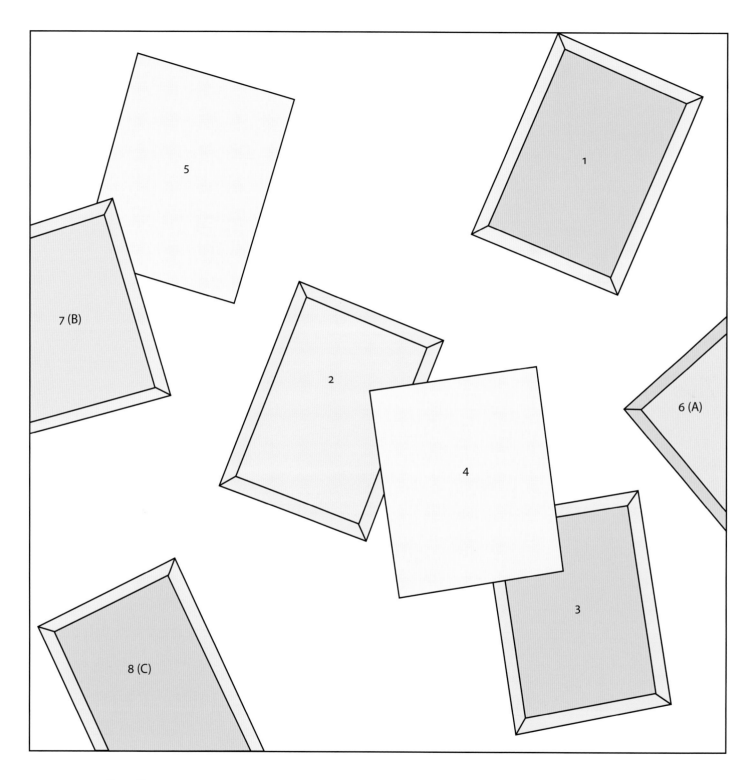

Adding Dimension to the Background

I used a simple technique to add extra dimension and texture to my Karuta design. Since I had more yardage than I needed of the fabric I chose for the background base, I decided to give my quilt a "layered" effect. I cut out 6" squares from the extra yardage, selecting a favorite section of the original pattern. I folded in the raw edges by ¼" all around, then appliquéd these squares onto the background base. This was done before adding any of the card appliqués. Look carefully at the photograph and you will see that the lighter colored squares at the top left and bottom left corners are slightly raised out of the background. I did the same with a darker section of the yardage at the bottom right of the quilt.

YOU WILL NEED

Background base: 16" × 16"

Backing: 16" × 16"

Batting: 19" × 19"

Side borders, cut 2: 5" × 20"

Top/bottom borders, cut 2: 5" × 16"

Cards and card frames: Scraps of at least 10 different fabrics

Use templates on page 114, adding seam allowances indicated.

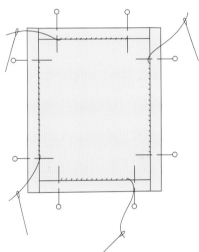

Prepare base

1. Prepare the background base following the steps on page 10 and using the layout diagram as a guide.

2. For cards 1, 2, and 3, cut rectangles measuring 3½" × 4½" from strongly patterned fabrics. Cut three same-size pieces of thin batting. Baste the batting to the back of each card. For the frames, cut three larger pieces, measuring 4½" × 5½". Pin each batting-backed card to the center of a frame frame piece. Fold the raw edges inwards by ½", then fold the turn-over inwards by ¼", allowing a ¼" frame to overlap the edges of the card. Press and pin. Beginning and stopping ½" from each corner, blind-stitch the frame to the card front around all edges. End with a double stitch, but leave the needle in place to continue later. For mitered corners, open out the fabric at each corner. Allow the fabric to come to a point at A, then fold point A inwards twice, manipulating the fabric until you have a nice, flat diagonal at the corner. Press, then continue to blind-stitch up to the corner, then diagonally across the miter. Complete cards 1, 2, and 3. Pin then appliqué each in place onto the background base, following the layout diagram.

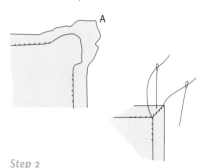

Step 2

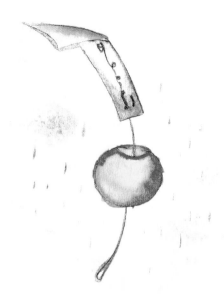

3. For cards 4 and 5, cut rectangles measuring 4" × 5" from fabrics that contain strong motifs. Depending upon the size of the motif you choose, your cards may vary slightly in size. Cut two pieces of thin batting measuring 3½" × 4½" (or ¼" smaller all around than your motif fabrics). Baste the batting to the back of each card. Fold the raw edges of the fabric inwards by ¼", overlapping the edges of the batting, and press. Position, pin, then appliqué cards 4 and 5 in place on the background base. Allow card 4 to overlap cards 1 and 2 as shown in the layout diagram.

4. Cut card 6 using template A (with no added seam allowance). Cut a same-size piece of batting and baste it to the back of the card. Add ½" around all sides of template A, then cut another piece of fabric for the frame. Pin the batting-backed card to the center of this frame piece. Along the two short sides, fold the raw edges inwards by ½", then fold the turn-over inwards by ¼", allowing a ¼" frame to overlap the edges of the card. Press. Miter the corners, as in Step 2. Position, pin, then appliqué card 6 onto the background base along the two short edges only. (There is no need to finish or sew the long edge, since it will later be disguised by the border).

6. For card 7, repeat step 4 using template B. This time, you will need to miter two corners. Position, pin, then appliqué card 7 onto the background base and

over the corner of card 5, as shown on the layout diagram. Prepare card 8 in the same way, this time using template C and mitering two corners.

Complete

7. See page 13 for directions on adding the backing and borders. Carefully position your borders to overlap the raw edges of cards 6, 7, and 8.

8. For the cards that overlap the quilt borders, find strong motifs in a fabric that complements the background base. Cut new cards to a size that showcases the motifs nicely. (My border cards measure about 5″ × 3″ when finished.) Cut the cards about ¼″ larger all around than the desired finished size. Turn under the raw edges and press. Appliqué over the finished border, overlapping to the back of the quilt, as desired.

A favorite memory is of my father writing letters. In my mind's eye, I see him holding in his hand a very thin brush soaked in Japanese *sumi* ink, writing a letter directly onto *makigami*, a long sheet of special paper that would roll up into a scroll. It seems like a very long time ago. I mostly remember my father as a man who was always hard at work, busy in the photo studio he owned. When I conjure the memory of him writing letters, I sense that this was a rare moment of peace for him. I imagine he was writing to my mother, who lived far away and whom he had not seen for a long time.

Japanese people no longer write letters on *makigami*, and even in stationery stores the scrolls and ink are hard to find. For my father, born during Japan's Meiji era, these graceful writing tools were a part of everyday life.

When I am tired and my thoughts are clouded, I often pick up my pen to write short essays or poetry. Writing works like medicine, allowing me to rest my mind and revitalize.

YOU WILL NEED

Background base: 16″ × 16″

Backing: 16″ × 16″

Batting: 19″ × 19″

Side borders, cut 2: 5″ × 20″

Top/bottom borders, cut 2: 5″ × 16″

Border accents: Two strips measuring 1½″ × 7½″; one each measuring 1½″ × 14¼″ and 2″ × 4½″

Scroll: Large scraps of at least two different fabrics

Leaves and buds: Scraps

Flowers: Scraps of at least four different fabrics

Sashiko thread or 2-ply embroidery floss

Use templates on pages 115–117, adding seam allowances indicated.

Prepare base

1. Prepare the background base following the steps on page 10 and using the layout diagram as a guide.

2. Select fabrics for the appliqués. Add seam allowances to the templates. Cut out and prepare all appliqué pieces (A to F) by folding under the seam allowances, then pressing and pinning each in place onto the background base. (Attach both parts to make a complete Template A.) Note that the larger pieces A to D require a ¼″ seam allowance, while E and F require just ⅛″. Appliqué A in place, then appliqué B to D on top of it.

3. Appliqué bud pieces E and leaf pieces F-1 to F-6 in place, setting the remaining F pieces aside.

4. Trace the sashiko designs (see sashiko templates on pages 34 and 35), then use embroidery floss or sashiko thread to stitch. Begin with the center vine, completing the longer lines of stitching with a continuous thread. When stitching the leaves, stitch the stems and center veins first. (See also page 11).

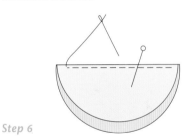

Step 6

Make nine flowers

5. Using template G, cut 18 circles from at least two fabrics. (I used four fabrics, cutting six each from the first pair and three each from the second pair.) Follow the directions on page 9 to prepare the circles for folding.

6. Fold the flower piece in half, then slide the top half back by about ⅜″. Press. Using strong thread, gather-stitch through all layers along the folded edge, leaving about ¼″ at either end.

7. Pull the gathers as tight as you can and make three or four stitches at point A to hold. Fold back the bottom layer. Attach to the background base by making a few stitches at point B and allowing the rest of the flower to hand free.

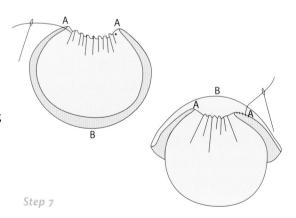

Step 7

Top-left vine

Center vine

Bottom-right vine

Step 4

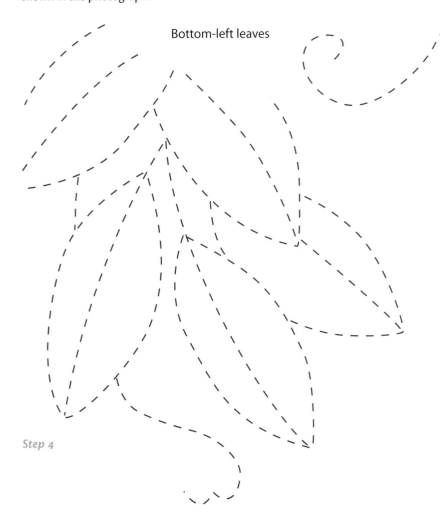

Complete

8. Prepare the border accent strips by folding in ¼" seam allowances, pressing and stitching in place on the border pieces (see also page 48). See page 13 for directions on adding the backing and borders. Appliqué leaf pieces F-7 and F-8 in place as shown in the photograph.

Left center vine

Bottom-left leaves

Step 4

I see cherry blossom covering the whole hill over there. How beautiful! Such a scene brings me many fond memories of springtime in the past.

桜咲き
丘いろづきて
思いあり

Spring

TSUBAKI

At the front door of the shrine where I lived with my aunt was a tall camellia tree surrounded by a thicket of kumazasa, a bamboo grass with large green leaves delicately rimmed with white. When the camellia flowers bloomed, their pink hues looked wonderful against this deep green background. In the backyard, there were two plum trees. When they were in flower, nightingales dressed in yellow and green feathers would visit to sing the arrival of spring. I would gaze at this lyrical scene in the afternoon sunshine.

A hundred stone steps away from the shrine where I lived as a child, there was the second shrine, with two surprisingly tall camellia trees growing outside it. The area was surrounded by a thick forest. Against a background of dark green glossy leaves that glinted in the sunshine lay deep pink camellia petals.

In this secluded place, I often played with a little boy, Takashi, who was two years younger than me. As winter gave way to spring, we two curious children would explore the countryside together, quenching our thirst with fresh spring water and making our own secret hiding place in a small cave close by. We would discover abandoned *hokura*, tiny alcoves among the rocks where people had made offerings long ago. Fallen camellia petals, piled up among the moss-covered *hokura*, impressed me with their natural beauty.

Images of those deep, mysterious woods and the echoes of fox calls at dusk are still vivid in my mind. Recalling them as I work on new designs, I relive moments of my childhood.

Camellia

TSUBAKI

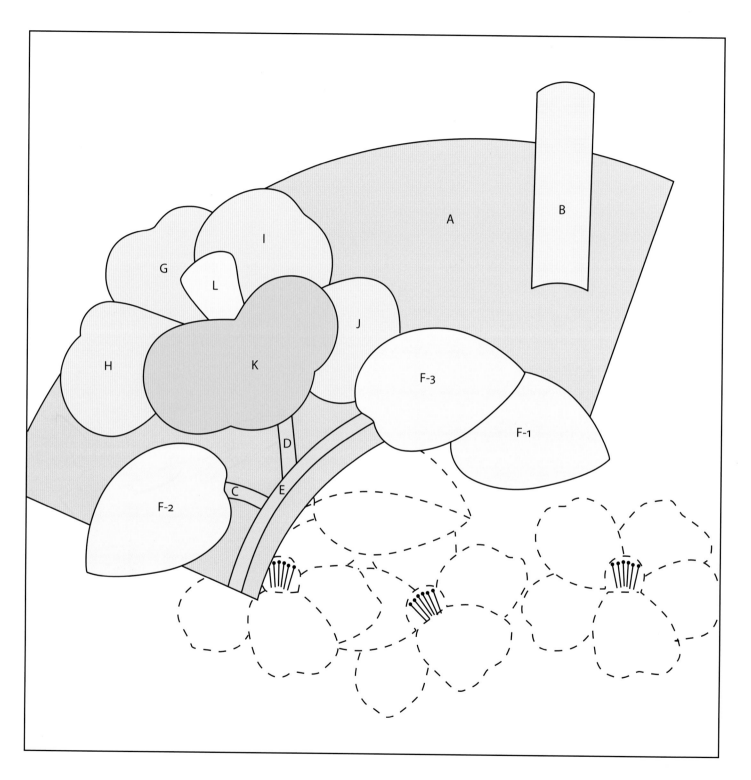

YOU WILL NEED

Background base: 16″ × 16″

Backing: 16″ × 16″

Batting: 19″ × 19″

Side borders, cut 2: 5″ × 20″

Top/bottom borders, cut 2: 5″ × 16″

Fan: Large scrap

Flowers: Scraps

Leaves and stems: Scraps

Sashiko thread or 2-ply embroidery floss

Use templates on pages 118–119, adding seam allowances indicated.

Prepare base

1. Prepare the background base following the steps on page 10 and using the layout diagram as a guide.

2. Select fabrics for the appliqués. Add seam allowances to the templates. Cut out and prepare all appliqué pieces (A to K) by folding under the seam allowances, then pressing and pinning each in place onto the background base. Note that the large fan piece A requires a ¼″ seam allowance, while all others require just ⅛″. Appliqué fan piece A in place.

3. Appliqué post piece B, stems C, D, and E, then leaf F-1 and F-2 (reverse). Appliqué flower pieces G, H, I, and J in place. Appliqué leaf piece F-3, overlapping as shown.

Make one bud

4. Using template L, cut one from each of two contrasting fabrics. Follow the directions on page 9 to prepare the pieces for folding. You may leave the bottom edge open.

5. Fold either side inwards by about ¼″ as shown. Press to hold, then appliqué the bud at the center of the flower. Appliqué flower piece K, trapping the bud in place and hiding the bottom raw edge.

Step 4

Step 5

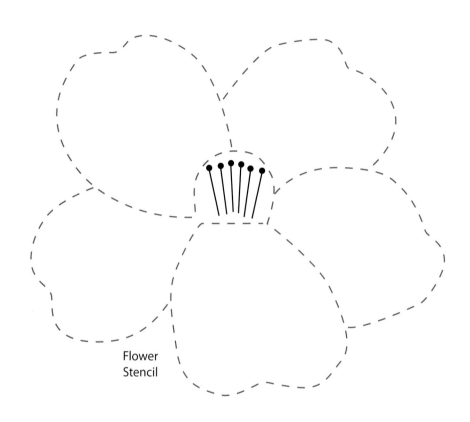

Flower
Stencil

Sashiko

6. Draw around template F (before seam allowance is added) to create the *sashiko* outline for the leaf, then stitch. Use the stencil to mark the flower pattern onto the background base, rotating the stencil to give each of the three flowers a slightly different appearance and overlapping them as desired. Stitch the semi-circle at the center first, then stitch the petals. To make the stamen pattern at the center of each flower, make extra-long stitches as shown. Begin by making a small, neat knot at the end of the thread. Working from the front to the back, carefully draw the thread through the fabric, allowing the knot sit on top of the fabric at point A. Take a very tiny stitch, exiting immediately below the knot. Draw the thread to point B. Insert the needle, exiting at C. Draw the thread to point D, insert the needle, take a very small stitch and come up immediately above the entry point. Make a very small knot as close the fabric as you can, so that the knot sits on top of the quilt front, then cut the thread. Repeat to complete the next two stamens and again to complete the fourth and fifth stamens. For the last stamen, make a small knot on the quilt front at E, take a very small stitch, then draw the thread to F. Knot off on the quilt back.

Step 6

Complete

7. See page 13 for directions on adding the backing and borders.

Tokyo's famous Kameido Tenjin Shrine is celebrated for its wisteria flowers. Ancient trees, their branches sweeping gracefully to the ground, have enchanted visitors for more than 600 years. The branches of the wisteria tree grow horizontally and the flowers clusters hang downwards like a veil of soft purples and lilacs. In spring, families picnic beneath the trees and stroll around the

Flowering Wisteria

MANKI NO FUJI NO HANA

grounds of the shrine, enjoying the beauty and the fragrance of these glorious flowers. When the wisteria are in bloom, vendors put up stalls at Kameido Tenjin and other shrines around Japan. They sell dolls, toys, and sweets reminiscent of wisteria. Happy families carry home souvenir branches of handmade silk wisteria flowers, adding to the excitement of new visitors who are approaching the shrine and heading for the wisteria trees.

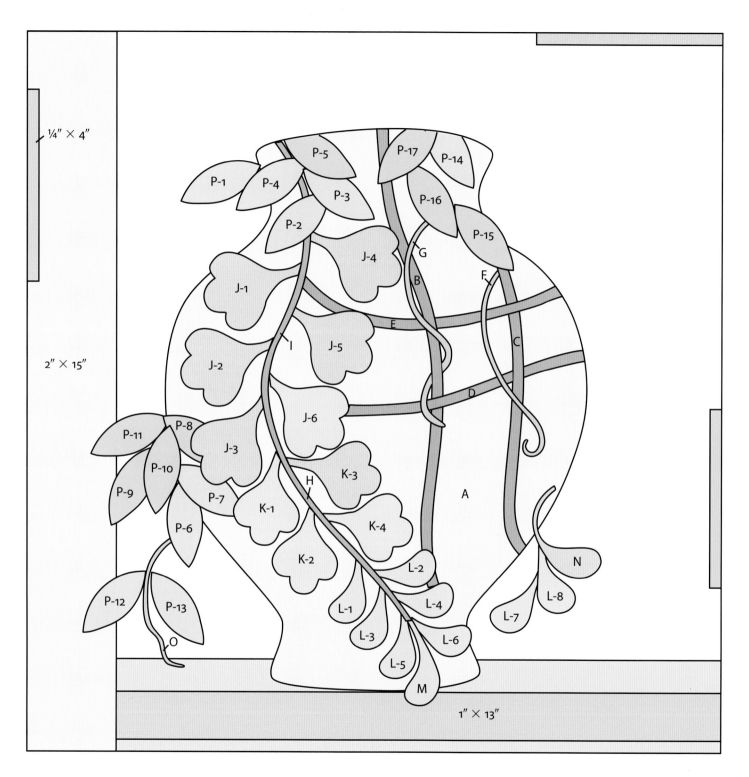

¼" × 4"

2" × 15"

1" × 13"

YOU WILL NEED

Background base: 16″ × 16″

Backing : 16″ × 16″

Batting: 19″ × 19″

Side borders, cut 2: 5″ × 20″

Top/bottom borders, cut 2: 5″ × 16″

Side inset border: 3″ × 16″

Layered bottom inset border:
    3″ × 14″, plus 2″ × 14″ strip in
    complementary fabric

Vase: ⅛″ yard or large scrap

Fence: Scraps of brown fabrics

Flowers, stems, and leaves:
    Variety of scraps

Logs: Small strips of colorful
    patterned fabrics

2-ply embroidery floss

*Use templates on pages 120–122, adding
seam allowances indicated.*

Prepare base

1. Prepare the background base following the steps on page 10 and using the layout diagram as a guide.

2. Fold one of the long raw edges of the wide bottom inset border strip inwards by ½″. Align the unfolded edge with the raw edge along the bottom of the background base and pin in place. Appliqué the border strip to the background base along the folded edge only. Fold both long edges of the other strip inwards by ½″ and press. Pin in place on top of and running across the middle of the first strip. Appliqué along both long edges.

3. Fold one of the long raw edges of the side inset border strip inwards by ½″. Align the unfolded edge with the raw edge along the left of the background base and pin in place. Appliqué the border strip to the background base along the folded edge only. At the bottom of the quilt, this border strip will overlap the Step 2 border strips.

4. Select fabrics for the appliqués. Make a complete vase template by joining the two sections of template A as indicated and adding ¼″ seam allowance. Appliqué vase piece A in place at the center of the bordered background base.

Border Accents

5. Add seam allowances to the templates, then cut out and prepare fence pieces B to G by folding in and pressing the seam allowance to hold. Position and pin each piece onto the vase appliqué. Begin to appliqué piece B, starting at the top of the vase. Stop at the point where this strip intersects with fence piece E. Leave the needle and thread in place. Repeat with piece C, this time beginning at the bottom edge and stopping where the strip intersects with fence piece D. Appliqué piece D in place, weaving it beneath C and stopping where the strip intersects with piece B. Finish appliquéing piece C, taking care to trap the top end of narrow vine strip F beneath C. Appliqué piece E in place, starting at the right edge of the vase and weaving the strip over piece C and under piece B. Finish appliquéing vine strip F. Appliqué a little more of strip B, weaving it over piece E. Continue for about 1", then stop. Begin appliquéing narrow vine strip G in place, weaving over B twice, then under the unsewn section of B. Finish appliquéing piece B, weaving over piece E. Finish appliquéing piece D, weaving over piece B. Complete vine strip G.

6. Prepare narrow vine strips H and I by folding in and pressing the seam allowance to hold. Position and pin each piece onto the vase appliqué. Do the same with all flower pieces K and J and bud pieces L and M. Begin to appliqué vine strip H in place, starting at the top of the vase and stopping where it intersects with the first flower piece. Appliqué the flower piece, then continue with the vine. Continue until all six J flowers, all four K flowers, six L buds, and the M bud are all in place. (Note: you will need to leave portions of flowers J-3 and K-1 unstitched until you have completed step 8.)

7. Appliqué the remaining buds (L-7 and L-8), then add bud N. Appliqué vine strip O.

8. Prepare leaf pieces P by folding in and pressing the seam allowance to hold. Position and pin each piece onto the vase appliqué. Appliqué P-1 through P-17 in place, overlapping as shown in the layout diagram. Complete the unsewn portions of flowers J-3 and K-1, overlapping leaf pieces P-7 and P-8.

9. Use embroidery floss and stem stitch (see page 12) to add curved tips to vine strips F, G and O. Begin with stitches of about ⅛" or the width of the vine tip, then decrease in size as you complete a pretty curve. Add an embroidered vine tip at the far right of the vase, immediately above the three-bud vine, as in the photograph.

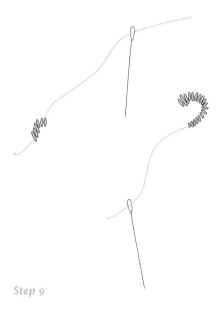

Step 9

Complete

10. See page 13 for directions on adding the backing and borders.

When I was just five, my older brother, who was a third-grade black belt in Judo, was my hero and I put all my confidence in him. Along with other neighborhood boys, my brother liked to play a game called "top fight"—a battle between spinning tops. The boys would start their tops spinning at the same time. The top that knocked rival tops over or sent them spinning into the circle of children crowding around to watch was the winner. I would stand outside the ring of older, taller children, my eye on my brother's top and my heart pounding. I always expected my brother to win, but top fighting requires great skill and this did not happen often. My brother's downhearted expression after losing at "top fight" is one of the most tender memories of my childhood.

Spinning Tops
KOMA

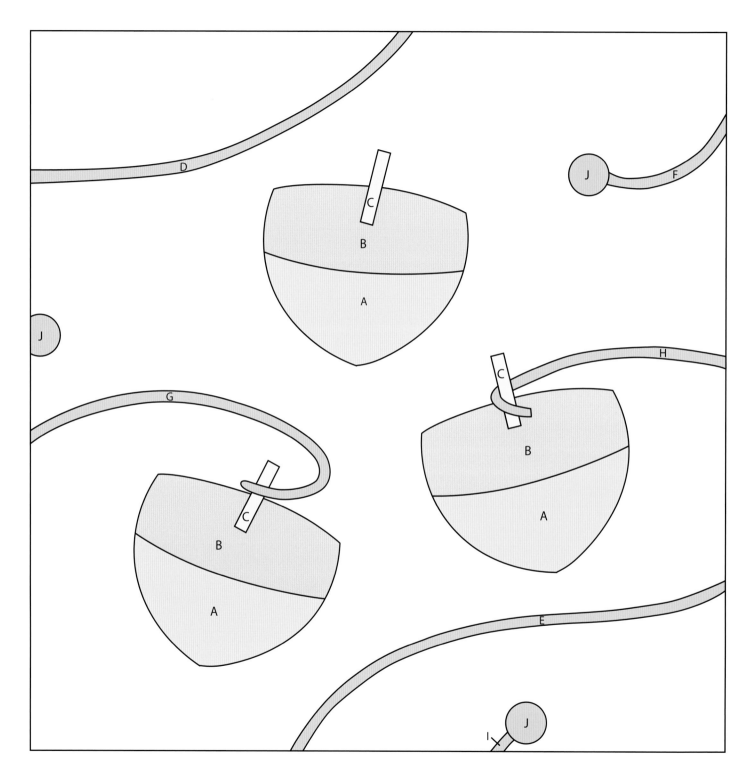

YOU WILL NEED

Background base: 16″ × 16″

Backing: 16″ × 16″

Batting: 19″ × 19″

Side borders, cut 2: 5″ × 20″

Top/bottom borders, cut 2: 5″ × 16″

Spinning tops: Scraps of at least 6 different fabrics

Whips and knots: Scraps

Use templates on page 123, *adding seam allowances indicated.*

Prepare base

1. Prepare the background base following the steps on page 10 and using the layout diagram as a guide.

2. Appliqué top pieces A then B in place.

3. Appliqué piece C at the top center of each spinning top, extending about ½″ into the top, as on the layout diagram. For the right-most spinning top, do not finish sewing piece C to the background base yet. Sew it only to the spinning top then leave the needle in place to continue later.

4. Position then pin whip pieces D, E, and F in position. Appliqué in place. Pin then appliqué whip piece G, sewing it in place over piece C on the left-most spinning top. Carefully position and pin whip piece H, looping the hook end behind the not-yet-sewn piece C on the right-most spinning top. Stitch it in place, then continue sewing piece C over it and onto the background base.

Replicating Multi-Design fabrics

Though at first glance my spinning tops may seem to be made from three or even four different fabrics, they are, in fact, made of only two pieces—A and B. I was lucky to find decorative fabrics that blend two or more colorations and designs into a single piece. Look, for instance, at piece B in the spinning top at the right of the photo (a detail is shown here). Printed as a single piece, this exquisite silk features a lovely band of purples, blues, greens and reds below a sea of solid tan; a narrow strip of orange separates the two designs, nicely curving to the shape of the spinning top. If you are unable to find multi-design fabrics like these, it's easy to recreate them. Choose two or three complimentary fabrics. Trace the desired template, adding a curved line at the point where you wish to break the design. Cut along your marked line to create two separate templates. Add ⅛" seam allowance around each one, then cut your fabric as usual.

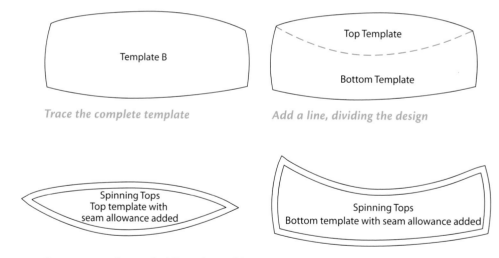

Template B

Trace the complete template

Top Template

Bottom Template

Add a line, dividing the design

Spinning Tops
Top template with
seam allowance added

Spinning Tops
Bottom template with seam allowance added

Cut apart at the marked line, then add seam allowance to each piece

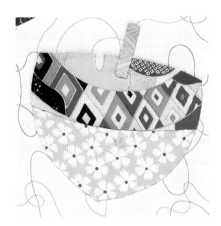

5. Complete the appliqués by stitching whip piece I and the three knot pieces J in place. Position the left-most knot carefully, so that it will be partially hidden by the quilt border.

Complete

6. See page 13 for directions on adding the backing and borders. Carefully position your borders to overlap the ends of whip pieces and the left-most whip knot.

Prince Hikaru Genji is the main character in *The Tale of Genji*, one the world's oldest novels, written by court lady Murasaki Shikibu. The novel depicts the aristocratic culture in Japan's Heian era through stories of emperors and nobles and their way of life. The word *ko* means aroma or incense. When *Genji* and *ko* are combined to make *Genji-ko*, the term refers to a sophisticated game involving incense that is based on *The Tale of Genji*.

Genji-ko requires 25 packets of incense—five packs of each of five aromas. For each round, five packets are randomly drawn from a bag. One by one each of the five samples is lit in an incense pot and circulated among the players. Each player inhales each aroma and tries to identify it, marking lines on a piece of paper according to a special scoring system to record his or her best guess. The line drawings that result from each round create a design.

The complex scoring system, which characterizes this game, involves 52 five-line designs. Each design corresponds to a chapter in *The Tale of Genji*, which in turn describes a particular character or place. To win, players must have considerable knowledge of poetry, classical literature, seasonal motifs, and Japanese history.

Heian-era nobles, including Prince Hikaru Genji, held elegant incense parties at the royal court. As I worked on this quilt design, I could almost hear the mirthful conversations between Prince Genji and the graceful ladies of the court, as the gentle scent of cherry blossom petals wafts through the air.

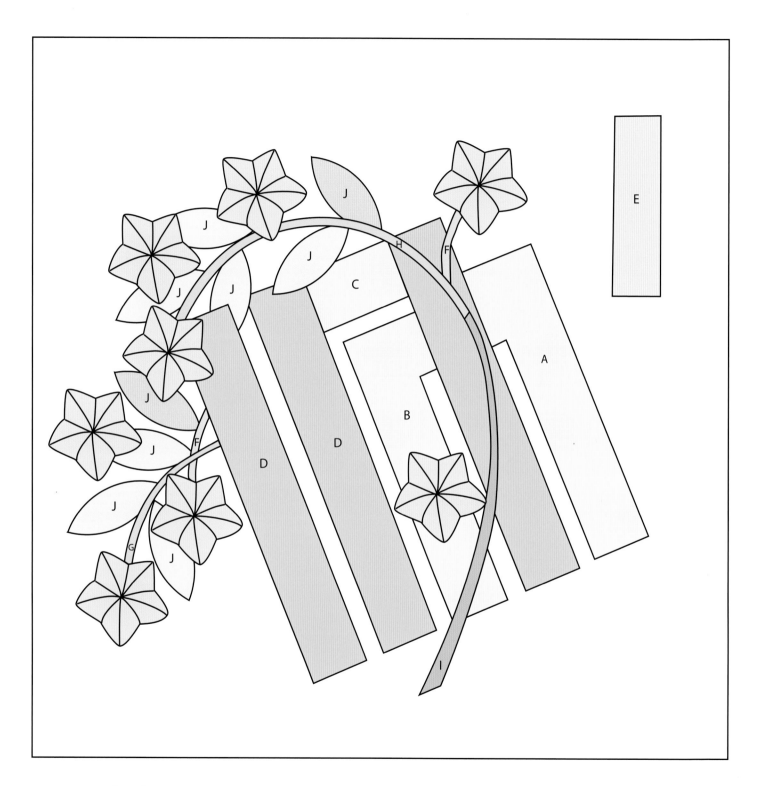

YOU WILL NEED

Background base: 16″ × 16″

Backing: 16″ × 16″

Batting: 19″ × 19″

Side borders, cut 2: 5″ × 20″

Top/bottom borders, cut 2: 5″ × 16″

Partition: Scraps of at least three different fabrics

Flowers: Scraps of up to ten different fabrics

Leaves and stems: Scraps of two or three different fabrics

Use templates on page 124, adding seam allowances indicated.

Prepare base

1. Prepare the background base following the steps on page 10 and using the layout diagram as a guide.

2. Select fabrics for the appliqués. Add seam allowances to the templates. Make templates C, D, and E by cutting rectangles measuring 2½″ × 1¾″, 1¾″ × 8½″, and 1½″ × 4¼″. (These measurements already include ¼″ seam allowance.) Cut out and prepare all appliqué pieces (A to J) by folding under the seam allowances, then pressing and pinning each in place onto the background base. Note that the large partition pieces A to E require a ¼″ seam allowance, while the stems and leaves need just ⅛″.

3. Appliqué partition pieces A to E in alphabetical order. Any edges that will be covered by a subsequent appliqué may be left unstitched.

4. Appliqué stem pieces G to I in place, followed by leaves J.

Make eight flowers

5. Using template G from *Bamboo Blind* (see page 130), cut 16 pentagons from a variety of different fabrics. Sort the pieces into contrasting pairs. Follow the directions on page 9 to prepare the pentagons for folding.

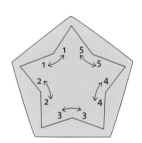

6. With the inside fabric facing, mark dots at ¼" inwards from each angle. Mark dots at ⅝" inwards from the midpoint of each pentagon side. Draw lines to connect the dots, creating a star shape at the center of the pentagon. With the diagram as a guide, fold line 1 to line 1 and use a running stitch to sew though all layers. In the same way, fold line 2 to line 2, 3 to 3, 4 to 4, and 5 to 5, stitching the sides of the star together.

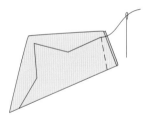

Step 6

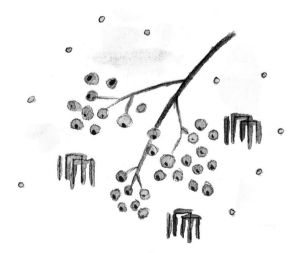

7. "Flatten" the flower, by pushing up from the base so that a pentagon shape is recreated and the inner tips of all five petals are at the center top (A). If necessary, add a stitch or two at A to make sure the inner tips are snug against each other. Fold back each side of each petal, wrapping the outer tip to the back. Use an awl or a chopstick to make each fold neat, precisely creating the flower shape.

Complete

8. Cut a strip of fabric measuring 3″ × 4½″ for the border accent. Turn under a ¼″ seam allowance. Sew the accent onto one of the vertical border pieces (see also page 48). Follow the directions on page 13 for adding the backing and borders.

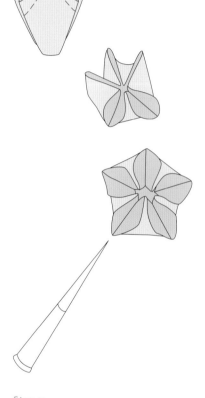

Step 7

During a spring breeze,
1 recall with nostalgia
the carefree moments
when 1 played in the water,
splashing droplets everywhere.

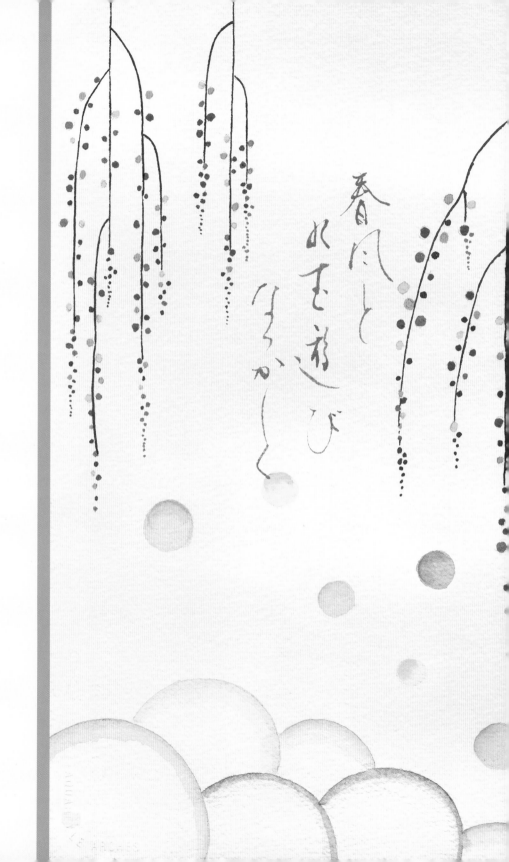

春風と
水を浴び
流かく

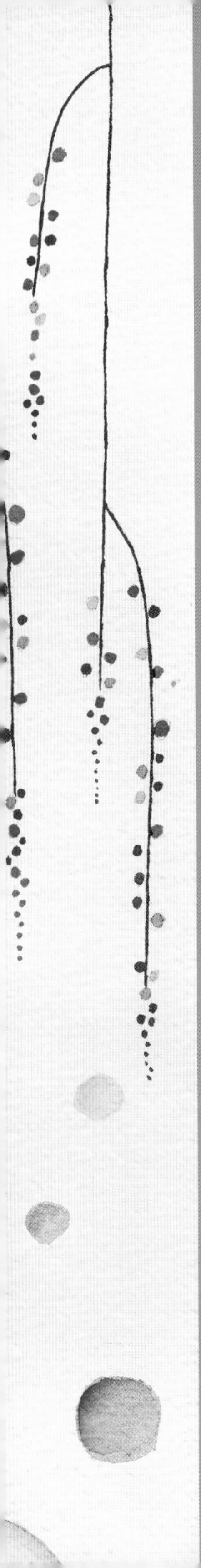

夏

Summer

NATSU

My aunt, who was a Shinto priestess in the Kamakura region of Japan, had close relationships with nuns at Buddhist convents and Zen monks at Kamakura Gozan, five high-ranking Zen temples in the area. Among her most beloved possessions was a kake-jiku that had been given to her by the monks at Enkaku-ji temple. She loved flowers and would always place a fresh seasonal arrangement in front of a kake-jiku selected to honor the season.

In early summer, open-air markets with everything from morning glories to wind chimes are set up on the grounds of temples and shrines all over Japan. The opening of the markets is a clear sign that the season is changing. Wind chimes, hanging from bamboo lattices, warn us of the oncoming heat of summer but at the same time remind us that gentle summer breezes will bring relief. When I was small, vendors on bicycles would pull carts laden with beautifully arranged morning glories through our neighborhood. The carts also held several round fish bowls, their rims fluted outwards like frills. Wind chimes hanging from a bamboo rod above them made lovely tinkling sounds as the vendors approached.

Wind Chimes

FUURIN

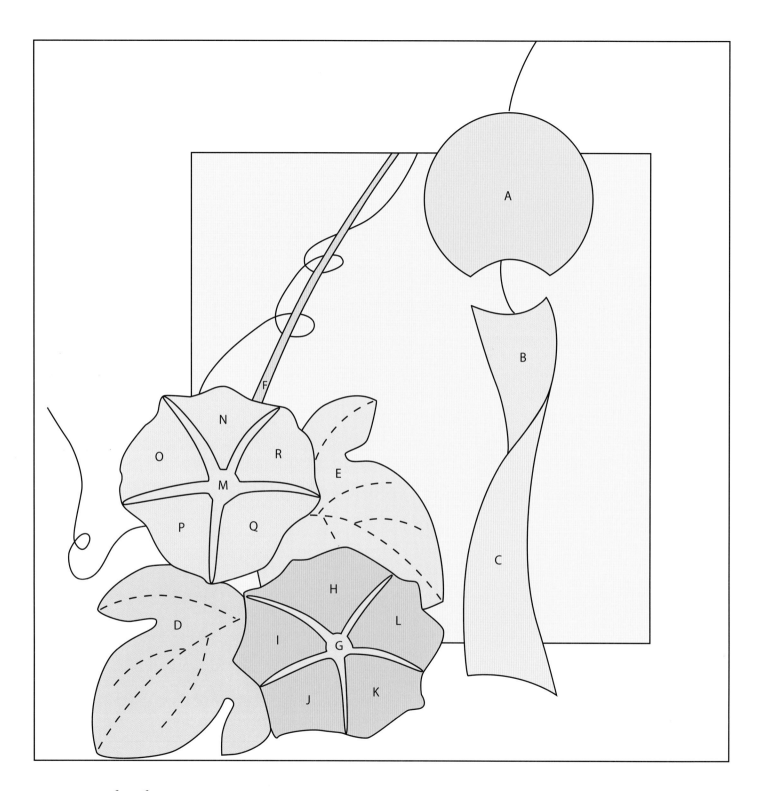

YOU WILL NEED

Background base: 16″ × 16″

Backing: 16″ × 16″

Batting: 19″ × 19″

Side borders, cut 2: 5″ × 20″

Top/bottom borders, cut 2: 5″ × 16″

Lattice: 1/4 yard or large scrap; small scrap
  of contrasting fabric

Wind chime: Scraps of multi-colored
  fabrics

Leaves and flowers: Scraps of multi-colored
  fabrics

Sashiko thread or 2-ply embroidery floss

*Use templates on pages 125–127, adding
seam allowances indicated.*

Prepare base

1. Prepare the background base following the steps on page 10 and using the layout diagram as a guide.

2. Cut a 10½″ square of fabric for the lattice. Turn in all edges by ¼″. Position the square 3¼″ inwards from the line marking the left border and 2″ inwards from the line marking the top border. Appliqué in place, leaving the bottom left corner unstitched since it will be covered with other appliqués.

3. Select fabrics for the appliqués. Add seam allowances to the templates. Cut out and prepare all appliqué pieces (A to R) by folding under the seam allowances. Press and pin pieces A to F in place onto the background base. You may need to snip the curves to make sure all pieces lie perfectly flat when pressed. Note that all pieces require a ⅛″ seam allowance.

4. Appliqué wind chime pieces A, B, and C in place. Appliqué leaf pieces D and E, then stem F.

5. Pin petal pieces H to L on top of flower piece G (right-most flower), wrapping the folded-in seam allowances of each petal around the edge of G. Appliqué each petal onto the flower piece, then appliqué the completed flower onto the background base. Repeat with petal pieces N to R and flower piece M.

Sashiko and Embroidery

6. Use the *sashiko* stencils marked on templates D and E or free-hand stitch veins onto the leaves, beginning with the center veins. (See also page 11).

Stem-Stitch Design

Stem-Stitch Design

7. Using stem stitch, embroider the twine as marked on the layout diagram. Where the vine intersects with stem F, simply push the needle beneath the fabric, exiting at the other side of the stem piece, then continue stem stitching.

Complete

8. See page 13 for directions on adding the backing and borders.

Nowadays *kiku* or chrysanthemums are sold at florists all year around, but when I lived in Japan flowers were available only when they were in season. For the Japanese, *kiku* are the hallmark of autumn. I love the scent of freshly grown chrysanthemums, and I have many fond memories of these flowers.

Each fall, I remember vendors pulling carts full of chrysanthemum pots through the streets. Unlike ordinary potted chrysanthemums that grow upright, these flowers were specially

Chrysanthemum Moon
TSUKI NI UTSURU KIKU

grown so that the stalks extended sideways over the pot by as much as three feet! They were tended as carefully as cultivated *bonsai*. My father would buy a potted chrysanthemum from the same vendor each year. He would display it in his photo studio, and my mother would place beside it a Japanese doll that she had handcrafted. The yellow chrysanthemum flowers with a touch of orange contrasted with the red floral patterns on the doll's kimono. The colors and aromas of late autumn filled the studio and, as young as I was, they put me into a reflective mood.

YOU WILL NEED

Background base: 16" × 16"

Backing: 16" × 16"

Batting: 19" × 19"

Side borders, cut 2: 5" × 20"

Top/bottom borders, cut 2: 5" × 16"

Moons: 1/4 yard or large scrap; small scrap of contrasting fabric

Leaves and stems: Scraps of multi-colored fabrics

Flower: Scraps for buds and flower center

Butterfly: Scraps of multi-colored fabrics

Sashiko thread or two-ply embroidery floss

Use templates on page 128, adding seam allowances indicated.

Prepare base

1. Prepare the background base following the steps on page 10 and using the layout diagram as a guide.

2. For the large moon, cut a 11"-diameter circle; for the small moon, cut a 4½"-diameter circle. (Both measurements include a ¼" seam allowance.) Select fabrics, then cut out all appliqué pieces (leaves A and B; petals C to I and stem to J for the left-most flower; and petals K to N for the right-most flower). Prepare them by folding under the seam allowances, then pressing and pinning each in place onto the background base. Note that pieces A to N require just ⅛" seam allowance.

3. Pin the large moon in place onto the background base. Look at the layout diagram to see where the leaf and petal pieces overlap the edges of the moon. Leaving these portions unstitched, appliqué around the rest of the circumference of the large moon. Appliqué the small moon in place.

4. Appliqué leaf pieces A and B in place. Add reverse piece B, tucking the right-most raw edge beneath the unstitched portion of the moon, then appliquéing smoothly around the curve.

5. Appliqué the left-most flower in the following sequence: petals C, D-1, D-2, E, F, G-1. G-2, G-3, G-4, H, I, then stem J.

6. Appliqué the right-most flower in the following sequence: petals K, L-1, L-2, L-3, L-4, M, L-5, L-6, then N. As you sew, tuck the bottom raw edges of each petal beneath the unstitched portion of the moon, then appliqué smoothly around the curve. Complete any remaining unstitched portions of the moon.

Sashiko

7. Transfer the *sashiko* designs onto the block (the leaf designs are marked on templates A and B). Use ⅛″ stitches for the background design and to outline-stitch around the small moon. Use smaller stitches to decorate leaves A and B. Each stitch should be about ¹⁄₁₆″, with ⅛″ space between the stitches (see also page 11).

Step 8

Make one chrysanthemum flower

8. For the petals, cut 40 squares measuring 2″ × 2″. Fold the top edge inwards by ¼″. Fold from A to B, then from C to D as shown and finger-press to hold. Wrap corner E around to the back and make a few stitches to hold in place.

9. Lightly mark a 1¾″ diameter circle onto the background base, exactly where you plan to position the flower center. Begin stitching the petals in place, positioning the raw edge at the perimeter of the marked circle. Sew a total of 22 petals around the circle, overlapping slightly as necessary to fit. Next, sew a second layer of 18 petals in place, this time positioning the raw edges about ¼″ inside the marked circle.

10. Cut a 2″ circle of fabric for the flower center. Fold under ⅛″ all round, then begin to appliqué the piece to the middle of the flower, covering all raw edges of the petals. When 1″ remains unstitched, stuff the flower center with batting or cotton scraps until it is firm. Stitch the opening closed.

Step 9

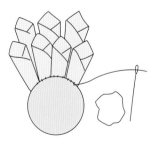

Step 10

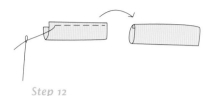

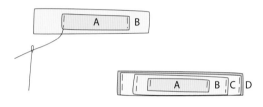

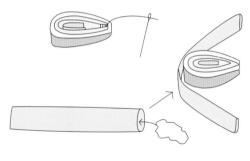

Butterfly

11. For the wings, cut the rectangles in the following sizes from multi-colored fabrics (each includes ⅛″ seam allowance).

A and F, cut 4: 2″ × 1″   E, cut 4: 4″ × 1¾″

B and H, cut 4: 3″ × 1½″   G, cut 2: 2″ × 1½″

C and D, cut 4: 3½″ × 1½″   I, cut 1: 3″ × 1″

12. Prepare wing pieces A, B, F, G, and two C pieces by folding each in half lengthwise, stitching along the long edges, and turning right side out to make "tubes." Press. Lay a very thin layer of same-size (or slightly smaller) batting on each of the two remaining C pieces and each E piece, then prepare in the same way as the other rectangles.

13. To make the upper wings, position A on top of B, stitching along the short ends to hold in place. In the same way, stitch C on top of a padded D, then sew the A/B unit on top of the C/D unit. Fold the combined units in half lengthwise, with A on the inside, and stitch across the raw edges. Make two or three additional stitches across the top of the layers to hold them firmly in place. Wrap padded piece E around this unit and stitch across the raw edge as shown. Make two upper wings.

14. For the lower wings, repeat step 13, this time stitching F on top of G and a remaining G piece of top of H. As before, combine units, then fold and stitch across the raw edges. Make two lower wings. (Notice that this time there is no padded layer to wrap around the wing.)

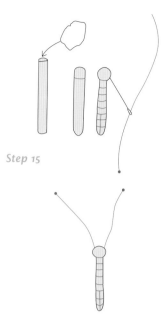

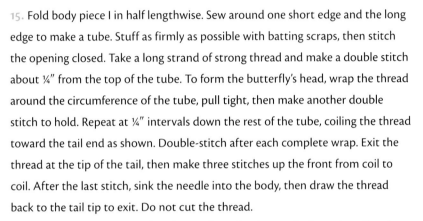

15. Fold body piece I in half lengthwise. Sew around one short edge and the long edge to make a tube. Stuff as firmly as possible with batting scraps, then stitch the opening closed. Take a long strand of strong thread and make a double stitch about ¼" from the top of the tube. To form the butterfly's head, wrap the thread around the circumference of the tube, pull tight, then make another double stitch to hold. Repeat at ¼" intervals down the rest of the tube, coiling the thread toward the tail end as shown. Double-stitch after each complete wrap. Exit the thread at the tip of the tail, then make three stitches up the front from coil to coil. After the last stitch, sink the needle into the body, then draw the thread back to the tail tip to exit. Do not cut the thread.

16. While there is still thread in the needle, poke the needle from the tail end along the full length of the body, exiting at the head, slightly right of center. Double stitch, then make a knot in the thread as close to the head as you can. Do not cut the thread. To form the antenna, make another knot about 2" further down the thread. Repeat to make the second antenna, this time slightly left of the center of the head.

17. Sew each set of upper/lower wing pieces together, then join them as shown. Sew to the underside of the body. Stitch the butterfly as desired onto the background base.

Complete

18. See page 13 for directions on adding the border.

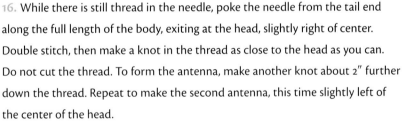

The sight of bamboo never fails to make me nostalgic for my childhood in Japan. A *misu*, or bamboo blind, always hung under the eaves of the Shinto shrine where my aunt, who was a Shinto priestess, lived. Originating in the palaces of the Heian period, when they were used as hanging partitions between rooms, Japanese bamboo blinds shut out direct rays from the sun while allowing soft light and air to filter through. *Misu* are made of narrow strips of bamboo only ⅛″ wide, joined together by fine strings and bound at the edges with silk brocade borders.

The *misu* at my aunt's house was more than a hundred years old. Tassels of linen threads dyed in white, red, and black hung from the bottom. I loved to watch it sway in the summer breeze with all its antique charm. While it shaded me from the hot afternoon sun, I loved to look through that *misu* and see the outlines of the mountain peaks that surrounded the house. Used by my family for more than a hundred years, my aunt's bamboo blind would transport me to an imaginary world of ancient people, towns, and villages. I still recall those late afternoons from the summers of decades past, and they are very dear to me.

Bamboo Blind

MISU

YOU WILL NEED

Background base: 16″ × 16″

Backing: 16″ × 16″

Batting: 19″ × 19″

Side borders, cut 2: 5″ × 20″

Top/bottom borders, cut 2: 5″ × 16″

Blind: Large scraps

Flowers: Scraps of four different fabrics

Leaves: 1⅛ yards (or at least 40″) of 3″-wide silk ribbon

Decorative cord: 2¾ yds (or at least 93″)

#25 embroidery floss (single ply)

Use templates on page 129–131, adding seam allowances indicated.

Prepare base

1. Prepare the background base following the steps on page 10 and using the layout diagram as a guide.

2. Select fabrics for the appliqués. Cut out and prepare all appliqué pieces (A to F) by folding under the seam allowances, then pressing and pinning each in place onto the background base. Note that the large scroll piece A requires a ¼″ seam allowance, while all others require just ⅛″. Mark the embroidery design onto piece A. You may use my kanji message or a message of your own creation.

3. Appliqué scroll piece A, then pieces B and C in place.

Decorative embroidery

4. Use stem stitch (see page 12) to embroider the marked kanji design onto piece A, stitching through both layers of fabric and the batting.

Decorative cord

5. Cut two 30″ lengths of cord and one 32″ length. Fold each length in half and finger-crease at the midpoint. (Note: in the diagrams, the left half of the cord is colored pink, while the blue half of the cord in colored blue, to make the steps involved in making the knot clear.) Pin the cord to a corkboard or a pincushion at this midpoint. Pick up cord end A (shown in pink) and make a loop, weaving over the cord and pulling end A through as shown. Pick up end B (shown in blue) and weave through the existing loop from front to back, then under the right-side (blue) cord. Pull end B through the new loop.

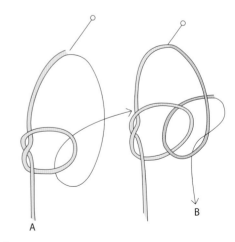

Step 5

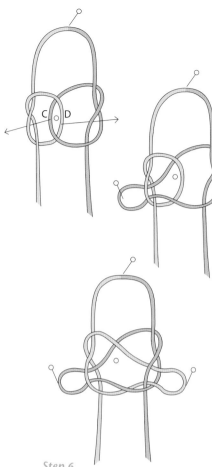

Step 6

Step 7

6. Place a second pin where the two center cords overlap, as shown. Pick up the cord at C (blue), then weave it through the left-hand (pink) loop. Pin to hold. Pick up the cord at D (pink), then weave it through the right-hand (blue) loop. Pin to hold.

7. Tighten the knot by tugging gently from the top and bottom, then from the side loops. If desired, make a stitch at the back to hold.

Continue background base

8. Position the two shorter knotted cords as shown in the layout diagram, at the top right and bottom right of the background base, arranging the loops and loose cord as desired. Use matching thread and stitch through the center of each cord, along its entire length.

9. Appliqué piece D, overlapping the cord as in the layout diagram. Appliqué piece E, leaving the top edge unstitched. Appliqué F-1 and F-2 in place. Note that since all the curved edges of D and E will be covered with other pieces, it is not necessary to appliqué these edges down. If you wish, you may leave them unstitched.

10. Tuck the left-most loop of the last cord (the longest one) beneath the open top edge of scroll piece E. Finish appliquéing piece E in place. Stitch the cord in place over piece E as in the layout diagram.

Make four flowers and four leaves

11. Using template G, cut two pentagons from each of four different fabrics. Sort the pieces into contrasting pairs. Follow the directions on page 9 to prepare the pentagons for folding.

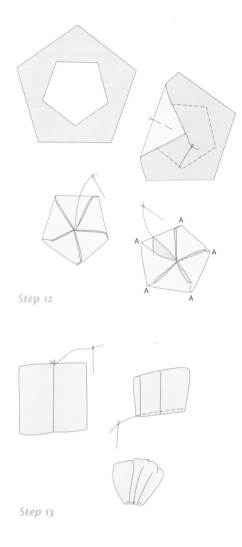

12. Cut template H from card and position it upside down on the sewn A pentagons as shown. Mark around the perimeter then set H aside. Fold one point of fabric pentagon A inwards toward the center and stitch to hold. Pin then press the fold firmly. Working clockwise around the pentagon, fold, stitch at the center, then press each fold firmly. You will need to tuck the last fold under the first to complete a perfect small pentagon. Open each side at point A to reveal the inside fabric. Press the folded side firmly, Pin, then stitch at the center as shown. Sew each flower in place onto the background base.

Step 12

13. Cut eight 5″ lengths of 3″ ribbon. (Make sure you have at least 1″ of ribbon left over for step 15.) Sew the strips of ribbon together in pairs along one long edge. Fold each piece in half across the seam and gather-stitch around the raw edges at the bottom. Pull the gathers and stitch to hold. Do not cut the thread.

14. Using the same thread, sew each leaf onto the background base along the gathered edge. Notice that each of these raw edges will be tucked beneath a flower. If desired, make additional stitches to secure the outer section of each leaf in place.

Step 13

15. Cut scraps of 3″ ribbon into four ¼″ strips. Roll each from end to end and stitch to secure. Sew to the center of each flower. Notice that the raw edges give these flower centers a soft, natural texture.

Step 15

Complete

16. See page 13 for directions on adding the backing and borders.

Today, paper lanterns are most often seen transformed into lampshades to decorate Japanese homes and gardens. But when I was little, lanterns were common household items—except at festival time, when the served a special role. Many a summer or autumn evening, I would look on with mounting excitement as my father or brother lit tiny candles inside our lanterns. During late-summer festivals, a lantern bearing the Chinese character for *matsuri* (which means festival) hung in front of every house, and people young and old would feel their heartbeats quicken at the sight of them. On the first night of the festival as the sun went down, the lanterns would light up one-by-one through the neighborhood, gradually turning ordinary streets into beautifully illuminated avenues.

The lanterns lit during the midsummer festival of *obon* are an especially lovely sight. During *obon*, Japanese people light lanterns to welcome the spirits of their ancestors back to their homes. The lanterns might be covered with silk, delicately hand-painted with pictures of seven species of flowers in light blues and greens. When they are lit, fantastic images dance in the lantern light, bringing comfort to all who see them. On the last evening of *obon*, square lanterns called *tōro* are set afloat in the rivers of Japan, and people believe they will find their way to the ocean to carry bright light to departed souls.

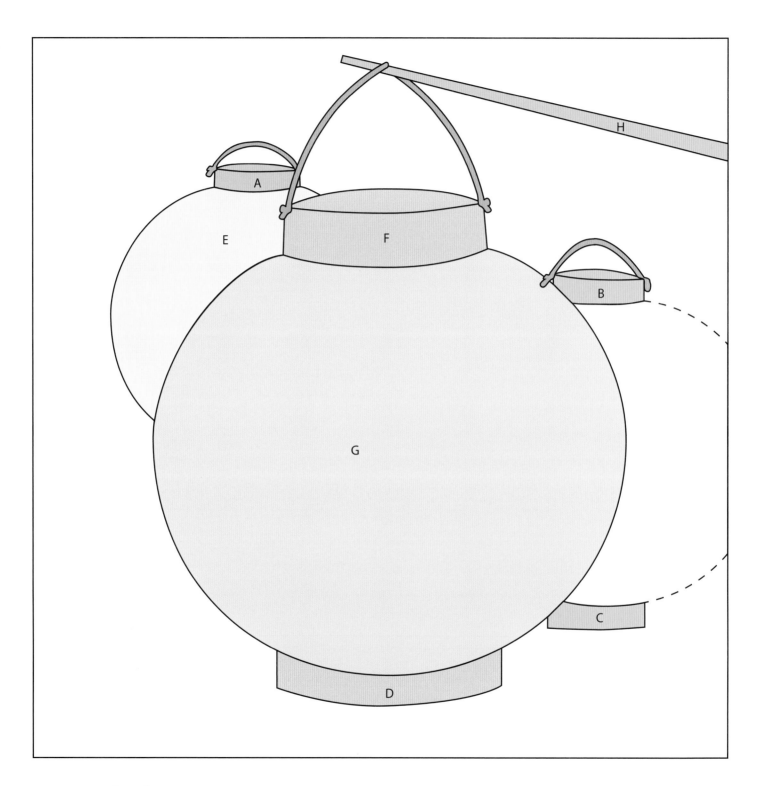

Prepare base

1. Prepare the background base following the steps on page 13 and using the layout diagram as a guide.

2. Select fabrics, then cut out and prepare all appliqué pieces (A to H) by folding under the seam allowances, then pressing and pinning each in place onto the background base. Note that the larger pieces E and G require a ¼" seam allowance, while all others require just ⅛". Notice, too, that top pieces A, B, and F are made from a single piece of fabric. If you do not have dual-design fabrics like these, make your own by following the directions on page 54.

3. Appliqué top and base pieces A to D in place. Next appliqué lantern piece E, followed by top piece F. Last, appliqué large lantern piece G, overlapping the other pieces as shown.

4. Begin appliquéing stick piece H, starting at the border edge and stopping with the last 2" unstitched. Leave the needle and thread in place.

YOU WILL NEED

Background base: 16" × 16"

Backing: 16" × 16"

Batting: 19" × 19"

Side borders, cut 2: 5" × 20"

Top/bottom borders, cut 2: 5" × 16"

Lanterns: Large scraps of two contrasting fabrics

Lantern bases and tops: Scraps of three or four different fabrics

Lantern handles: ½" yard decorative cord

Sashiko thread or 2-ply embroidery floss

Stick: Scrap

___

Use templates on pages 132–133, adding seam allowance indicated.

5. Cut the decorative cord into one 8" length and two 5" lengths. Make knots at either end of each one. Stitch the two shorter cords in place, looping from side to side of top pieces A and B. Begin stitching the 8" cord, beginning at the right edge of top piece F and weaving under stick piece H. Finish appliquéing stick piece H, trapping the cord in place. Loop the cord over the end of the stick and continue stitching it in place.

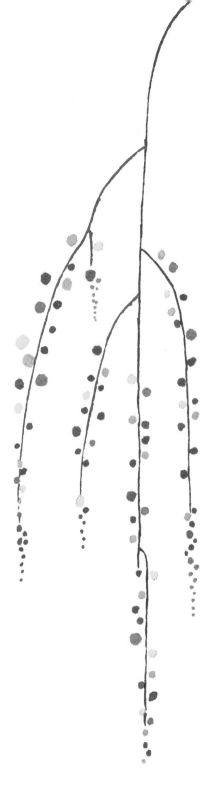

Sashiko

6. The body of the third lantern, at the far right of the quilt, is created not from templates but by two curved lines of *sashiko* stitching. Use colorful *sashiko* thread or embroidery floss to create both lines, prior to adding the backing and borders. (See also page 11).

Complete

7. See page 13 for directions on adding the backing and borders. Notice that I used two contrasting fabrics for the vertical/horizontal borders.

The image of birds flying home against the glow of the sunset is so beautiful. It reminds me of myself in old times running home after playing with friends.

夕暮の
向うに見ゆる
とぶ鳥の
姿をしも
我身見ゆる
里に

Autumn

AKI

The Shinto religion teaches that all living things have spirits, and the beautiful illustrations in Kake-Jiku capture that teaching. When we admire a kake-jiku, we do so in a way that honors the spirit it depicts. Seeing a drawing of a hawk, we might say, "It looks as though it is just about to take flight," or we might react to a painting of plum blossoms with, "I enjoy the drifting fragrance."

As a grade-school student I lived with my aunt, deep in the mountains of Kamakura. Each autumn day, when summer recess was over, I would make the long walk alone to school, carrying my bright red satchel on my back. I enjoyed autumn breezes on my cheeks as I walked along a certain pathway shaded by the overhanging branches of *hagi* trees, or bush clover. The trees grew on a rise, on the other side of a stone wall. Their branches reached out from behind the wall and their swaying tips were reflected in

Reading Under the Vines
SHIDAREHAGI NO SHITA NO DOKUSHO

the waters of a creek that flowed down below. Sudden gusts of wind would blow hundreds of flower petals into the air, sending them soaring into the blue autumn sky that was spotted with white clouds. Some fell into the creek and slowly floated away, and I caught others in the palm of my hand. The small deep pink petals were lovely and filled my heart with joy.

That pathway is my eternal friend. Even today, when I am reading or listening to music, I sometimes think back and I feel as though I am standing there among fallen *hagi* petals.

Prepare base

1. Prepare the background base following the steps on page 10 and using the layout diagram as a guide.

2. Select fabrics for the appliqués. Cut out and prepare all appliqué pieces (A to F) by folding under and pressing the seam allowances. Note that the larger piece A requires a ¼″ seam allowance, while B to F require just ⅛″.

YOU WILL NEED

Background base: 16″ × 16″

Backing: 16″ × 16″

Batting: 19″ × 19″

Side borders, cut 2: 5″ × 20″

Top/bottom borders, cut 2: 5″ × 16″

Book: ⅛ yard or fat quarter

Book cover: Scraps

Leaves and flowers: Scraps

Buds: ⅛″ silk ribbon, total of 1 yard in two or three different colors

Sashiko thread and/or two-ply embroidery floss

Use templates on pages 134–136, adding seam allowances indicated.

Repeat this grid
to cover entire piece A

Top

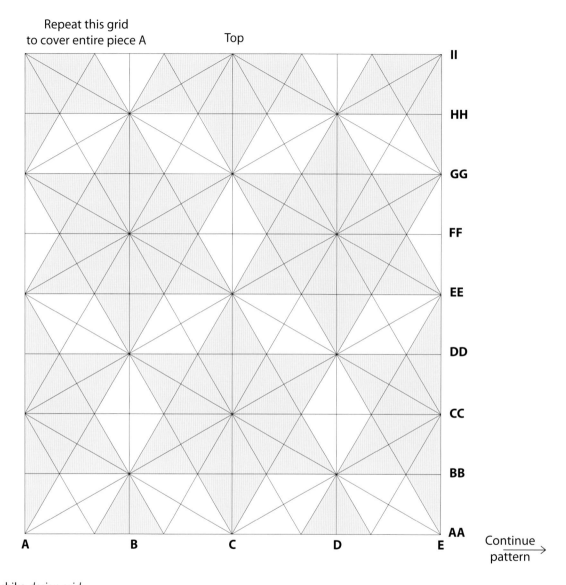

II

HH

GG

FF

EE

DD

CC

BB

AA

A   B   C   D   E

Continue
pattern →

Step 3 Basic sashiko *design grid*

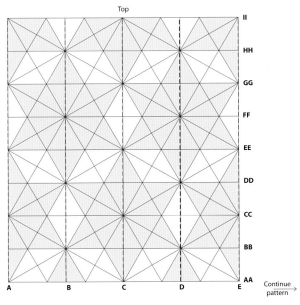

Step 4 *Vertical rows of* sashiko *stitching*

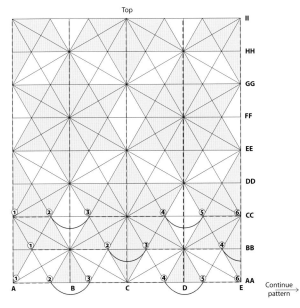

Step 5 *Horizontal rows of* sashiko *stitching*

Sashiko

3. Mark a ¼″ seam allowance around all sides of book piece A, then trace or copy the star *sashiko* design grid onto it. (The stencil shows just a portion of the design; you will need to repeat the design across the entire piece of fabric.)

4. Beginning at the bottom left, make a vertical row of stitches about 1⅛″ inwards from the raw edge (⅞″ inwards from the seam allowance) on the marked line. This is row A in the diagram. Repeat every 1⅛″ across the width of piece A on the marked lines, making a total of ten vertical rows of stitches. Note that due to the shape of piece A, the last, right-most row, will be a partial line of stitches.

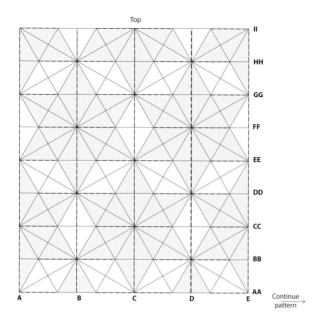

Step 5 *Horizontal and vertical rows completed*

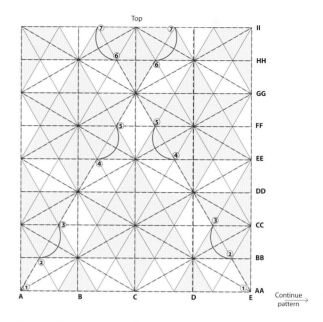

Step 6 *Diagonal rows of* sashiko *stitching*

5. Next stitch the horizontal rows. Beginning at the bottom left, stitch horizontal row AA until you reach the leftmost point of the first half-diamond (about ¾"). Insert the needle from front to back, exiting at the rightmost point of the same half-diamond. Continue stitching across row A, making large stitches at the back from left to right of each diamond as before. Complete all rows, noting that the placement of stitches is staggered in alternating rows.

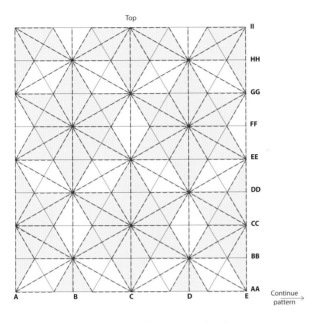

Step 7 *Remaining diagonal rows completed*

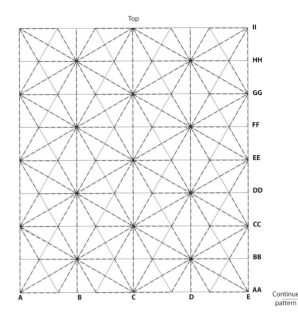

Step 7 *Complete*

6. To begin the diagonal rows, begin at the bottom right corner (AA) and stitch diagonally across the piece. (As before, you are drawing the thread across each diamond at the back of the work.) Complete all diagonal rows. Repeat, this time beginning the bottom left and working up to the top right.

7. Stitch the remaining diagonals on the grid (from C to CC, A to EE, etc.).

8. Changing thread color, make a vertical line of stitching through the center of the piece, from top to bottom, to delineate the center-fold of the book.

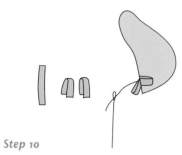

Step 10

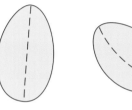

Step 11

Continue base

9. Appliqué book cover pieces B and C in place, (You will need to trim B-R.) Appliqué A, slightly overlapping the inner edges of B and C.

10. Cut the ribbon into 1″ lengths, for a total of 36 strips. Fold each in half and finger-press to hold. Appliqué bud pieces D in place, trapping the raw edges of folded ribbon strips in position as shown.

11. Appliqué leaf pieces E and F in place.

Decorative embroidery

12. Using the photograph and the layout diagram as guides, mark the vine pattern. Mark and stitch the long stems first, then the shorter stems. Use stem-stitch embroidery (see page 12) to complete the vine pattern. Continue stem stitch through the center of some of the leaves as shown.

Complete

13. See page 13 for directions on adding the backing and borders.

When I think of *sado* or the Japanese tea ceremony, I am often reminded of the great master of this art, Sen-no-Rikyu. As well as being a celebrated teacher, Rikyu was also a talented merchant, who was very successful in trading tea utensils. Tea bowls that Rikyu sold are highly valued today by those who are devoted to *sado*. Mastering the tea ceremony is believed to lead to an understanding of Zen teachings, and a master of *sado* is said to grasp the unlimited silence and infinity of the universe in a bowl of green tea.

Green Tea
RYOKUCHA

緑茶

Prepare base

1. Prepare the background base following the steps on page 10 and using the layout diagram as a guide.

2. Cut a 12½" diameter circle for the moon (includes ¼" seam allowance). Appliqué it onto the base. You may leave the bottom edge unstitched, trimming away any excess fabric so that the moon does not show below the tea cups.

3. Select fabrics for the appliqués. Add seam allowances to the templates. Cut out and prepare all appliqué pieces (A to F) by folding under the seam allowances, then pressing and pinning each in place onto the background base. You may need to snip the curves to make sure all pieces lie perfectly flat when pressed. Note that the large cup pieces C and D require a ¼" seam allowance, while all others require just ⅛".

4. Appliqué cup pieces A in place, leaving the lower edges unstitched. Appliqué B-1 and B-2 in place, leaving the upper edges unstitched. Appliqué C then D, covering the raw edges of the underlying pieces.

5. Appliqué B-3 in place, leaving the bottom edge unstitched (this will be covered by the border in step 6). Appliqué pieces E then piece F in place, replicating the shape of the left-most cup. Where these pieces extend over the border, leave those portions unstitched.

Sashiko

6. Using *sashiko* thread or embroidery floss, outline-stitch around the top edges of pieces E, around the outer edge of piece F, and along the short edges of piece B-3. Where the pieces extend into the border, leave those portions unstitched but keep the needle and thread in place. (See also page 11.)

Complete

7. See page 13 for directions on adding the backing and borders. Cut a border accent piece measuring 1¾" × 5¼". Turn under ½" seam allowance all round, then appliqué in place, overlapping the left border (see also page 48). Finish appliquéing pieces E and F onto the border, then complete the final line of outline-stitch on the outer edge of piece F where it overlaps the border.

YOU WILL NEED

Background base: 16" × 16"

Backing : 16" × 16"

Batting: 19" × 19"

Side borders, cut 2: 5" × 20"

Top/bottom borders, cut 2: 5" × 16"

Moon: Large scrap or fat quarter

Teacups: Scraps of at least two fabrics

Sashiko thread or 2-ply embroidery floss

Use templates on pages 137–138, adding seam allowances indicated.

A favorite Japanese folk tale of mine is *The Crane Who Returned the Favor*. This is how the story goes.

One day a kindhearted young hunter found an injured crane in the snow. He took it home and cared for it. When the crane's wounds were healed, the hunter set it free. A few nights later, a lovely woman knocked on the door of his cottage asking for lodging. The hunter and the woman fell in love and were married. The couple led a happy life, until one day the wife told the hunter that she was starting a new weaving project and asked him not to watch her while she was weaving. From the next day on, she locked herself in the barn and wove day and night. She only came out only to hand the hunter rolls of beautifully woven fabric, which were highly prized and sold for good prices. Although the hunter became wealthy, he missed his wife. Unable to resist his desire to see her, he peeped inside the barn through a crack in the wall. There he saw a ragged crane plucking its own feathers and weaving them on the loom. The lovely wife was that beautiful crane the hunter had rescued, and she had come to him to repay him for his kindness.

The story continues, but I would like you to read it for yourself. While Japanese folklore is filled with tales of sparrows, swans, ravens, and other creatures, the crane is the most beloved as a symbol of long life. It is a familiar motif in Japanese households and is almost always worked into the designs of bridal kimonos.

鶴

Crane

TSURU

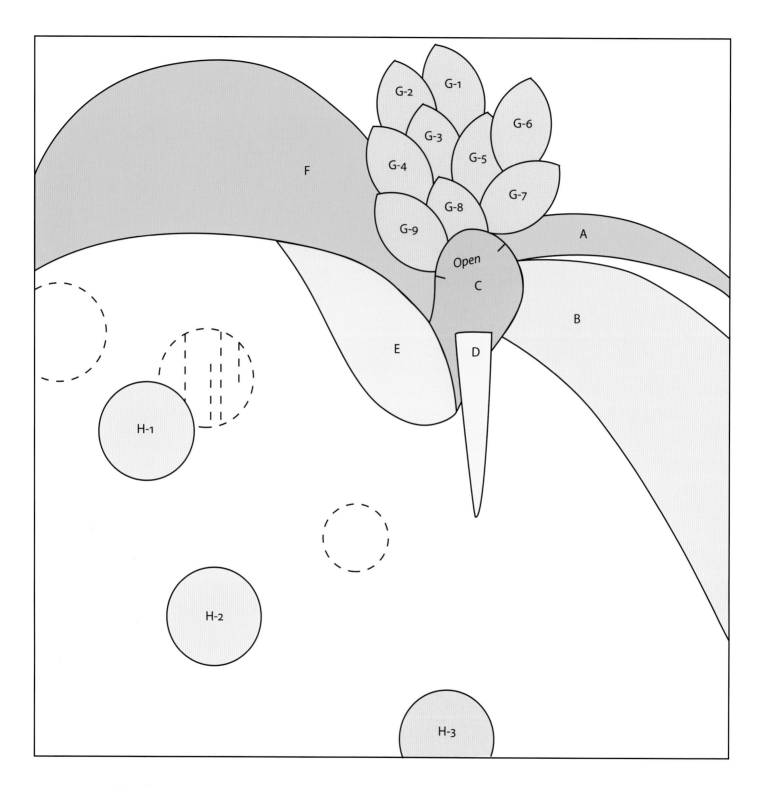

Prepare base

1. Prepare the background base following the steps on page 10 and using the layout diagram as a guide.

2. Select fabrics for the appliqués. Add seam allowances to the templates. Cut out and prepare all appliqué pieces (A to H) by folding under and pressing the seam allowances. Note that the larger pieces B and F require a ¼″ seam allowance, while the smaller pieces require just ⅛″.

3. Appliqué wing pieces A and B in place, then appliqué head piece C, slightly overlapping them. Leave unstitched the section of C marked "open" on the layout diagram. (You may leave the short edges of A and B unstitched, since these will be covered by C and by the border.)

4. Appliqué beak piece D, then wing E and body F in place. (As before, you can leave any raw edges that will be covered by subsequent appliqués unstitched.)

5. Appliqué feather pieces G in place in the sequence shown on the layout diagram. Tuck the short edges of G-8 and G-9 beneath C, then complete stitching C.

6. Appliqué circles H in place. You may leave the portion of H that will be hidden by the border unstitched.

Sashiko

7. Using *sashiko* thread or embroidery floss, outline stitch around fabric circles H. Mark then stitch two same-size circles (2″ diameter) as shown (both are incomplete circles), then stitch a smaller circle (1½″ diameter). Mark then complete the *sashiko* design. (See also page 11.)

8. If desired, using a thin-tipped fabric marker and a very light touch, copy the markings onto the background base, using the photograph as a guide. Practice first on paper, then work on the fabric.

Complete

9. See page 13 for directions on adding the backing and borders.

Background base: 16″ × 16″

Backing: 16″ × 16″

Batting: 19″ × 19″

Side borders, cut 2: 5″ × 20″

Top/bottom borders, cut 2: 5″ × 16″

Bird: Large scraps of three or more different fabrics

Buds: Scraps

Fabric marker (optional)

Use templates on pages 139–140, adding seam allowances indicated.

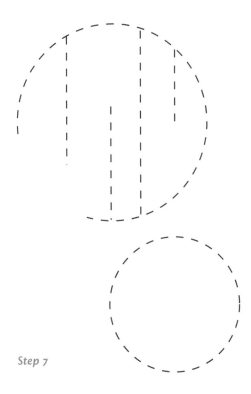

Step 7

Autumn | Crane 109

Templates

KATAGAMI

All templates are drawn to full size and do not include seam allowances. If you need a guideline for positioning templates on the background block, begin by tracing or photocopying the templates onto template plastic or stiff card. Transfer all labels and markings. Using tailor's chalk or another quilters' marker, lightly draw around each one onto the background fabric. Next, position each template on the fabric from which it is to be cut. Eyeball a ⅛" seam allowance (or the seam allowance indicated) around all sides and cut to size. If you are uncomfortable estimating the seam allowance, remake your templates with the seam allowance already added in. Remember that appliqué is very forgiving—if your seam allowance is slightly off, it will not be noticeable on the finished piece.

Note that many of the larger appliqués have been divided in order to fit onto the page (see *Letter Scroll* on pages 116–117, *Flowering Wisteria* on pages 120–121, *Bamboo Blind* on pages 129–130, and *Reading Under the Vines* on pages 134–136). Before marking or cutting, create the complete template by taping the separate pieces together as indicated on the templates.

Combs *see pages 18 to 19*

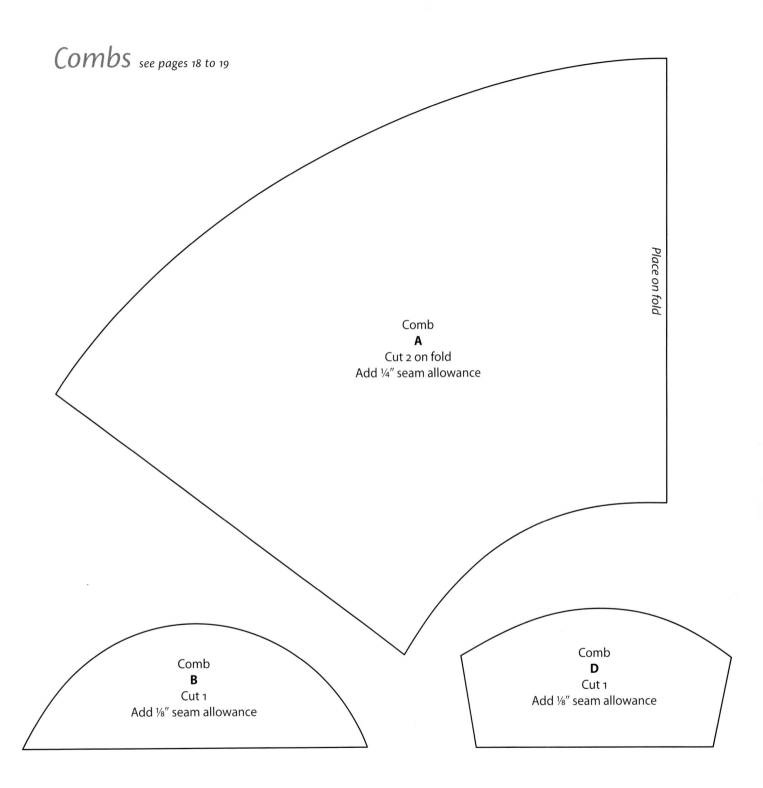

Place on fold

Comb
A
Cut 2 on fold
Add ¼″ seam allowance

Comb
B
Cut 1
Add ⅛″ seam allowance

Comb
D
Cut 1
Add ⅛″ seam allowance

Combs *see pages 18 to 19*

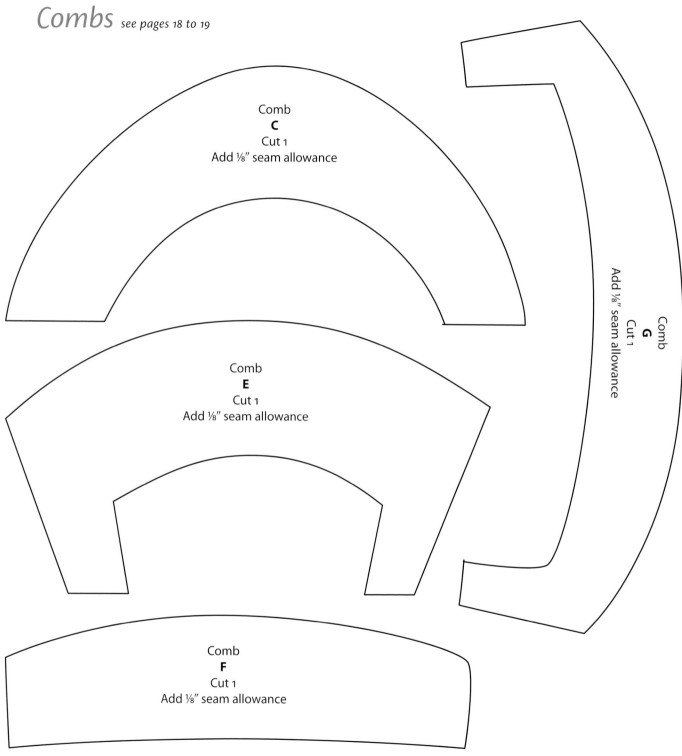

Comb
C
Cut 1
Add ⅛" seam allowance

Comb
E
Cut 1
Add ⅛" seam allowance

Comb
F
Cut 1
Add ⅛" seam allowance

Comb
G
Cut 1
Add ⅛" seam allowance

Battledore *see pages 22 to 23*

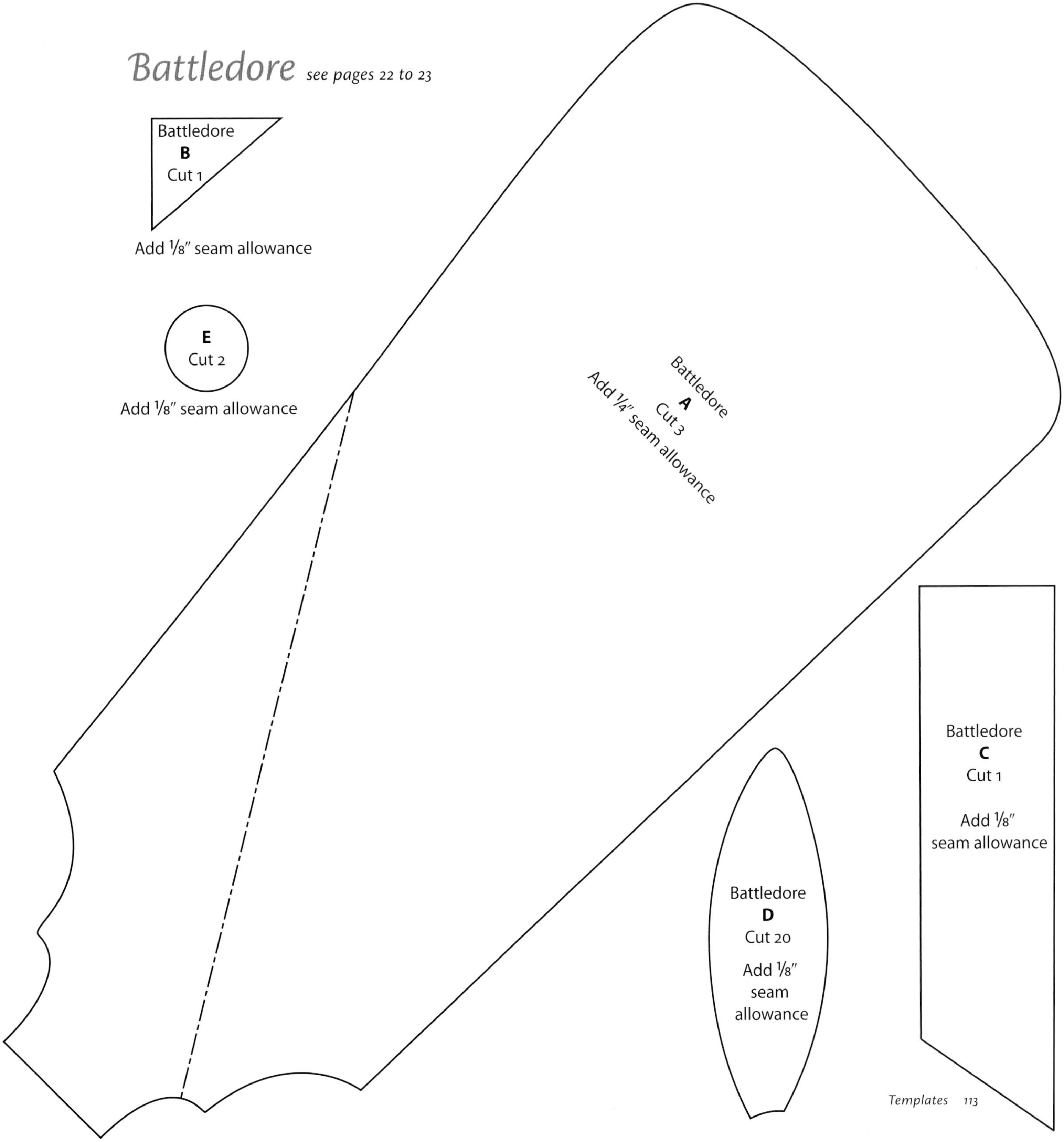

Battledore
B
Cut 1

Add ⅛″ seam allowance

E
Cut 2

Add ⅛″ seam allowance

Battledore
A
Cut 3
Add ¼″ seam allowance

Battledore
C
Cut 1

Add ⅛″
seam allowance

Battledore
D
Cut 20

Add ⅛″
seam
allowance

Karuta *see pages 26 to 29*

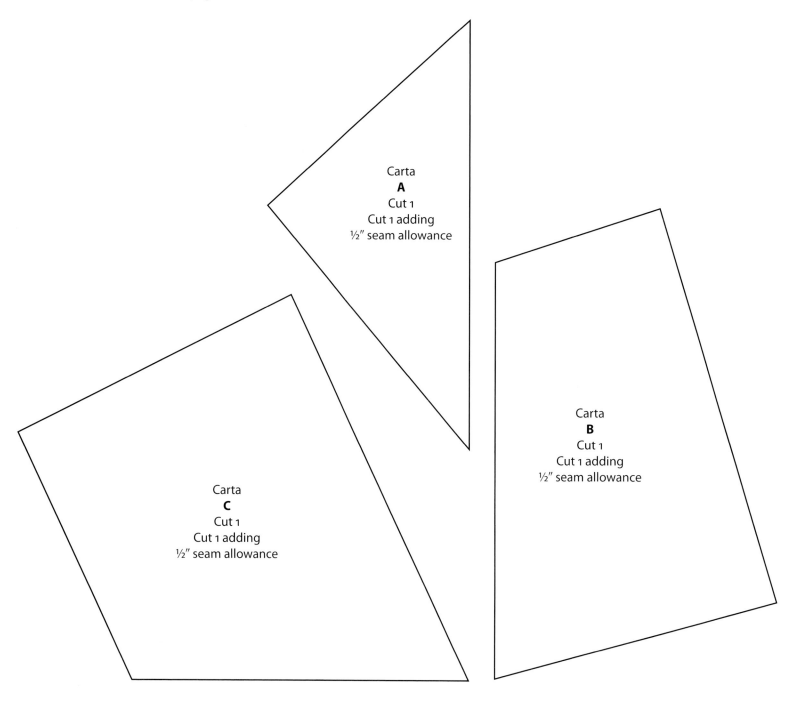

Carta
A
Cut 1
Cut 1 adding
½" seam allowance

Carta
B
Cut 1
Cut 1 adding
½" seam allowance

Carta
C
Cut 1
Cut 1 adding
½" seam allowance

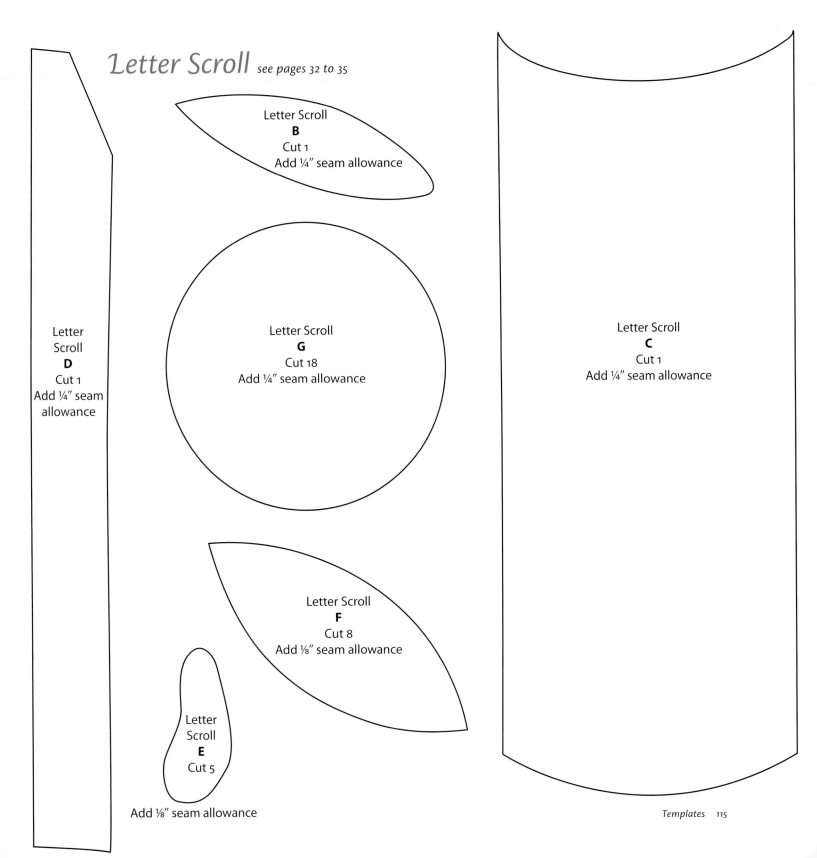

Letter Scroll see pages 32 to 35

Letter Scroll
B
Cut 1
Add ¼″ seam allowance

Letter
Scroll
D
Cut 1
Add ¼″ seam
allowance

Letter Scroll
G
Cut 18
Add ¼″ seam allowance

Letter Scroll
C
Cut 1
Add ¼″ seam allowance

Letter Scroll
F
Cut 8
Add ⅛″ seam allowance

Letter
Scroll
E
Cut 5

Add ⅛″ seam allowance

Letter Scroll

see pages 32 to 35

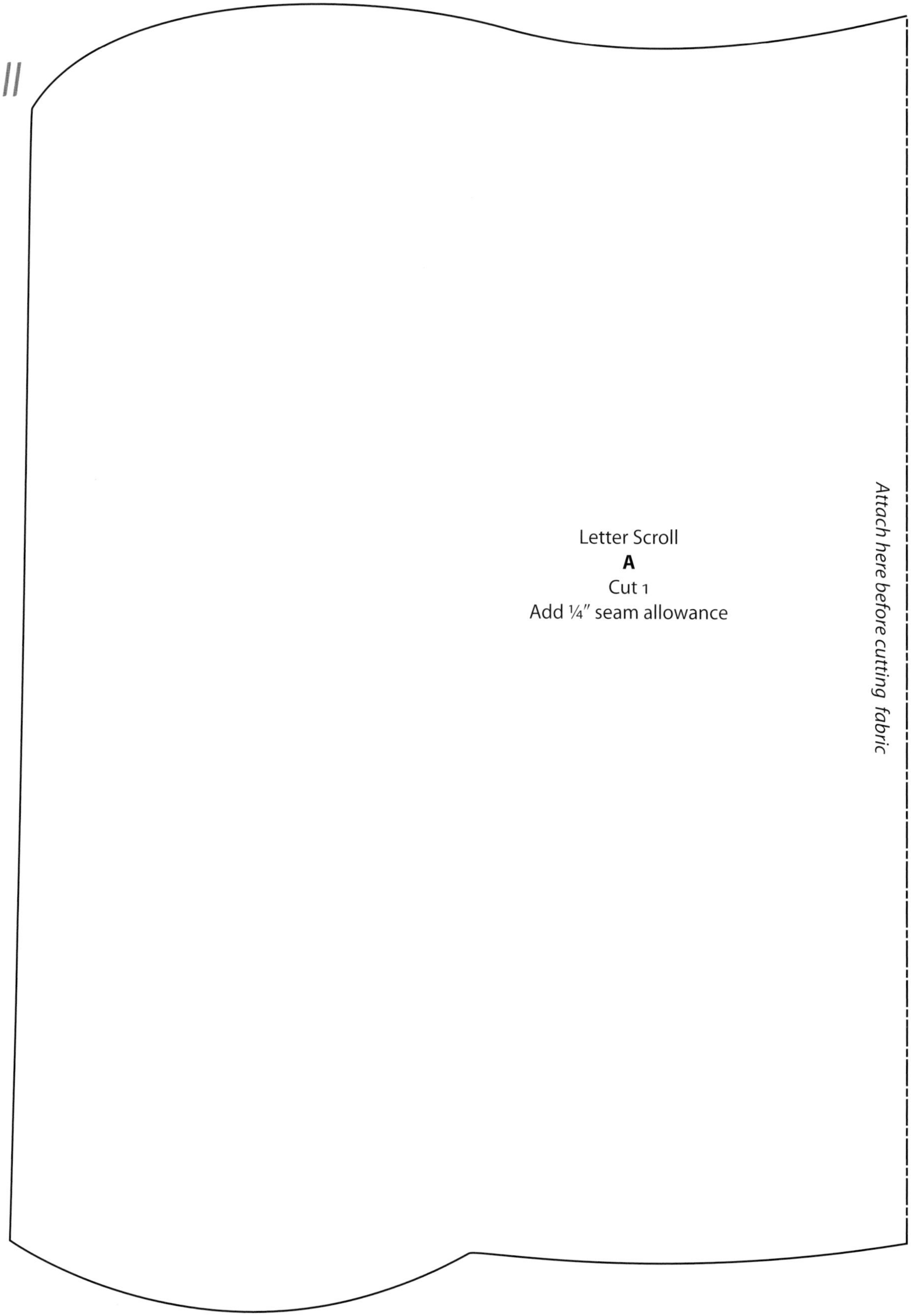

Letter Scroll
A
Cut 1
Add ¼" seam allowance

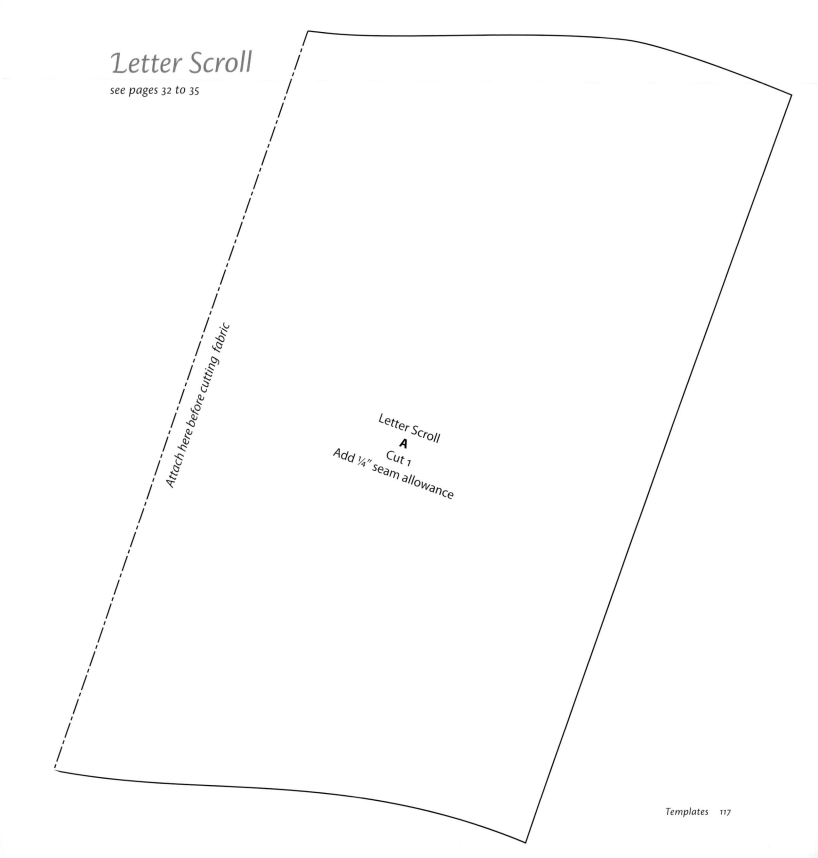

Letter Scroll

see pages 32 to 35

Attach here before cutting fabric

Letter Scroll
A
Cut 1
Add ¼" seam allowance

Camellia *see pages 40 to 43*

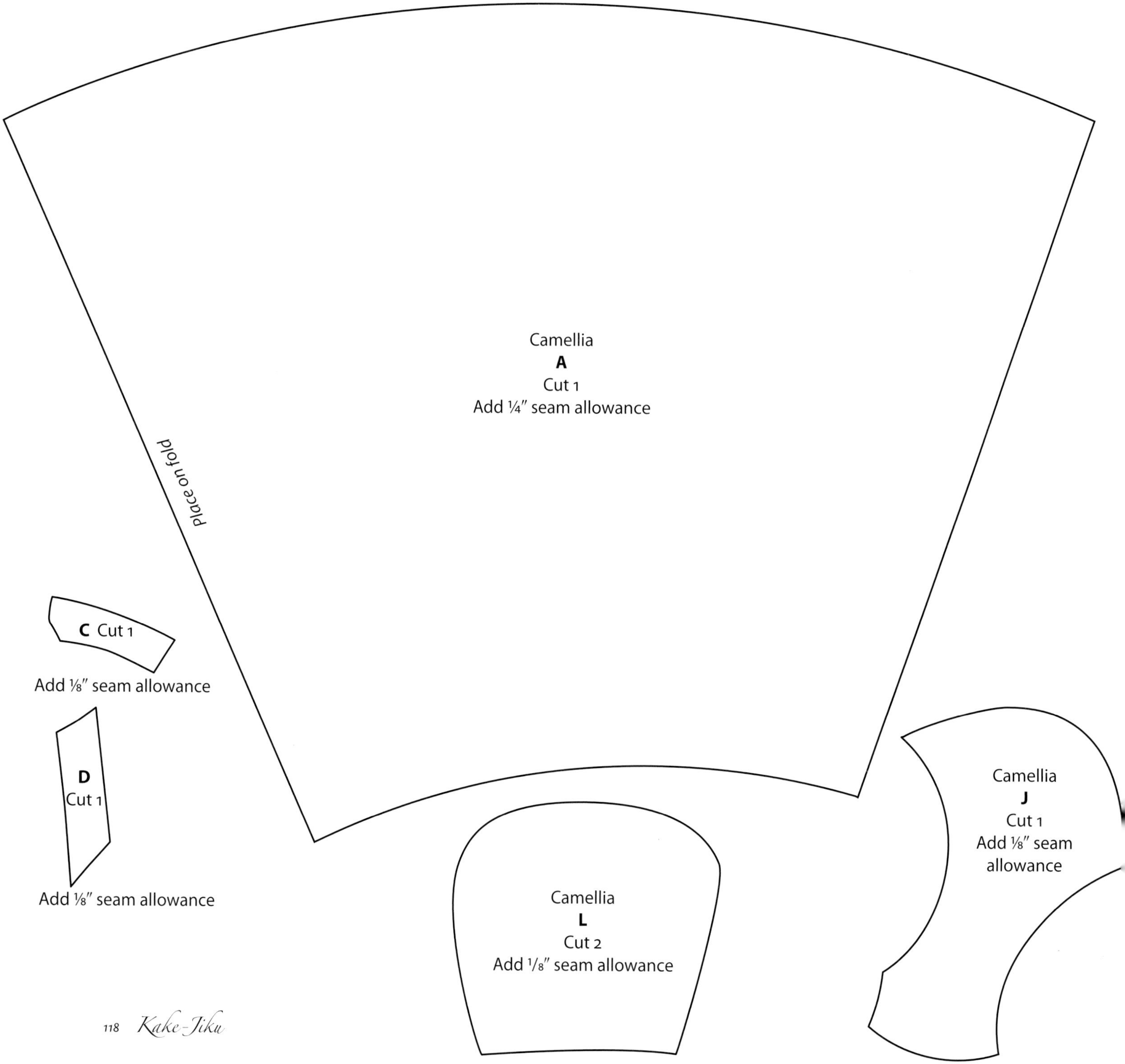

Place on fold

Camellia
A
Cut 1
Add ¼″ seam allowance

C Cut 1

Add ⅛″ seam allowance

D
Cut 1

Add ⅛″ seam allowance

Camellia
L
Cut 2
Add ⅛″ seam allowance

Camellia
J
Cut 1
Add ⅛″ seam allowance

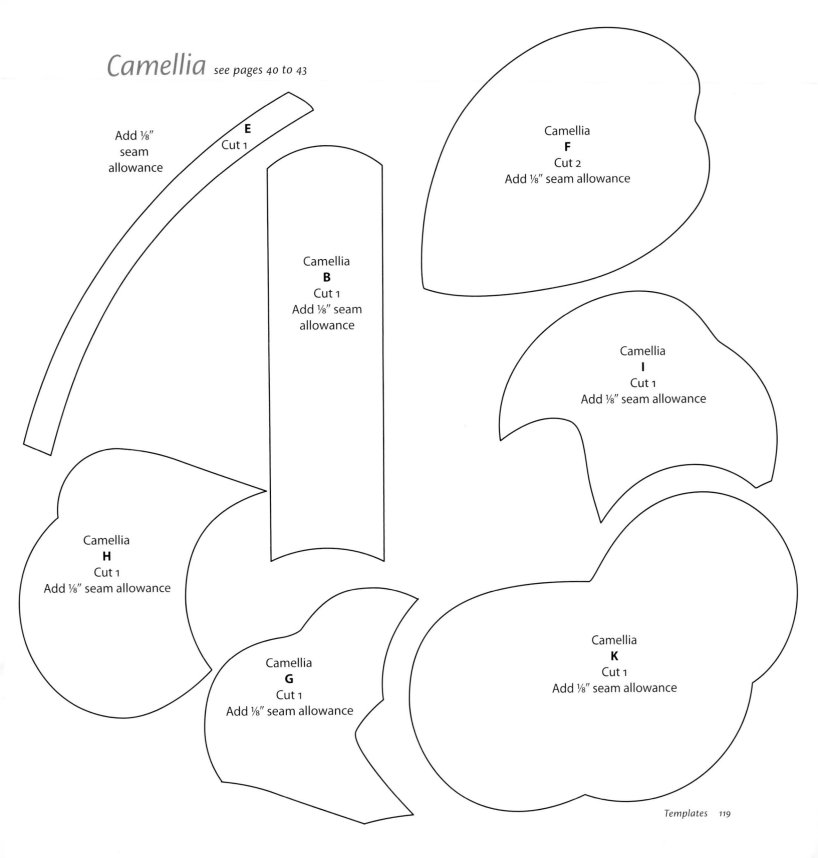

Camellia see pages 40 to 43

Add ⅛"
seam
allowance

E
Cut 1

Camellia
F
Cut 2
Add ⅛" seam allowance

Camellia
B
Cut 1
Add ⅛" seam
allowance

Camellia
I
Cut 1
Add ⅛" seam allowance

Camellia
H
Cut 1
Add ⅛" seam allowance

Camellia
G
Cut 1
Add ⅛" seam allowance

Camellia
K
Cut 1
Add ⅛" seam allowance

Flowering Wisteria

see pages 46 to 49

Top

Flowering Wisteria
A
Cut 1
Add ¼" seam allowance

Attach here before cutting fabric

Flowering Wisteria
K
Cut 4 *(Reverse for 2)*
Add ⅛" seam allowance

Flowering Wisteria
J
Cut 6 *(Reverse for 3)*
Add ⅛" seam allowance

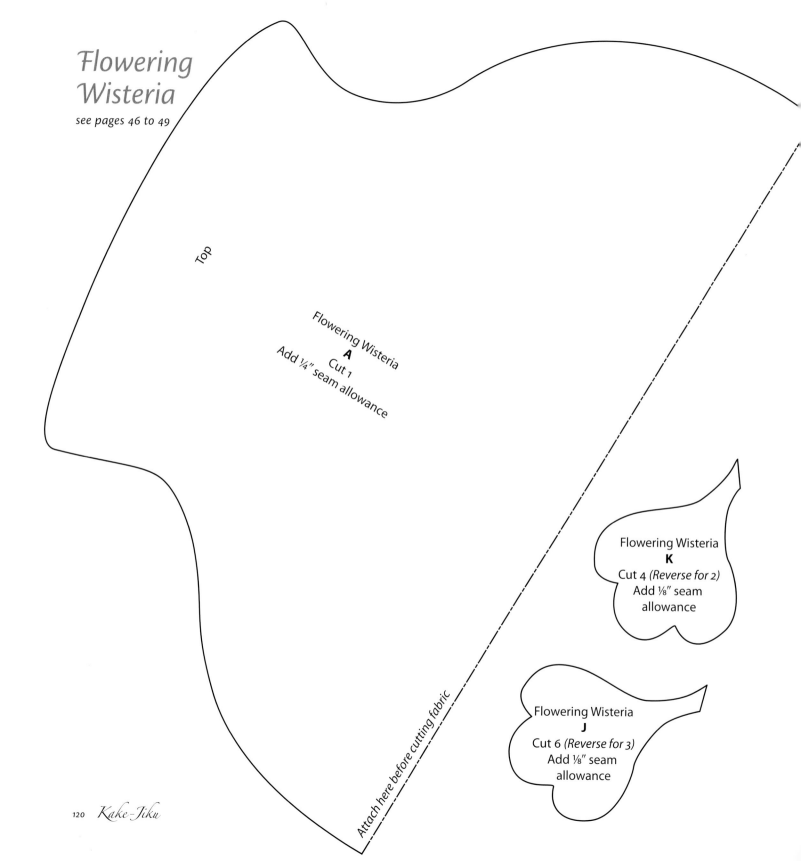

Flowering Wisteria

see pages 46 to 49

Attach here before cutting fabric

Flowering Wisteria
A
Cut 1
Add ¼" seam allowance

Bottom

Flowering Wisteria *see pages 46 to 49*

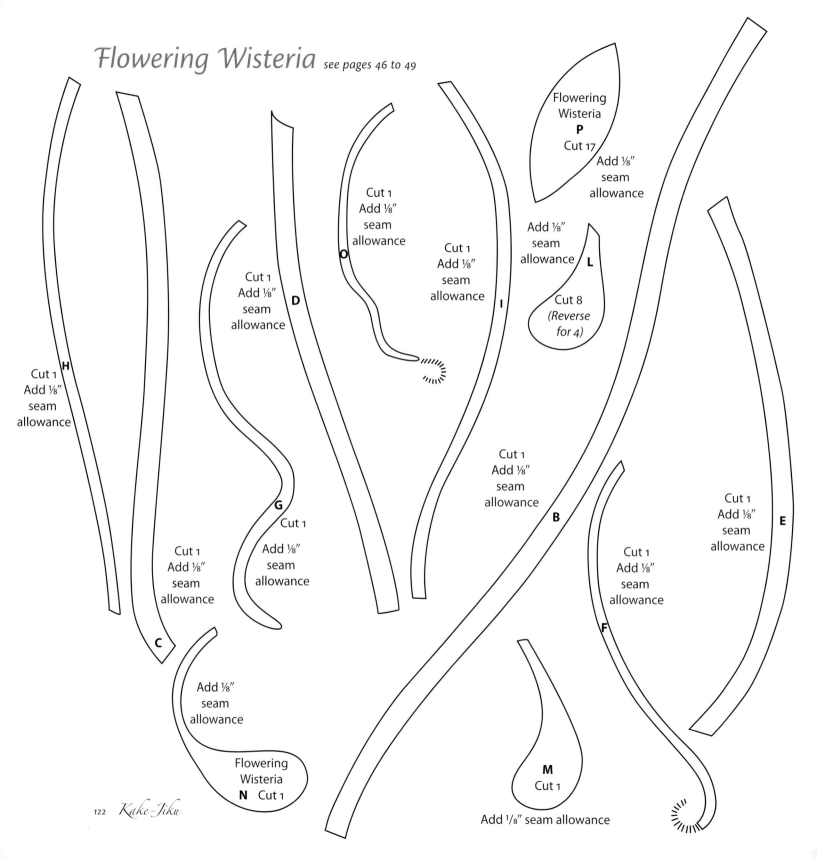

Flowering
Wisteria
P
Cut 17
Add ⅛″
seam
allowance

Cut 1
Add ⅛″
seam
allowance

O

Cut 1
Add ⅛″
seam
allowance

I

Add ⅛″
seam
allowance
L

Cut 8
*(Reverse
for 4)*

Cut 1
Add ⅛″
seam
allowance
D

Cut 1
Add ⅛″
seam
allowance

H
Cut 1
Add ⅛″
seam
allowance

Cut 1
Add ⅛″
seam
allowance

B

Cut 1
Add ⅛″
seam
allowance
E

G
Cut 1

Cut 1
Add ⅛″
seam
allowance

Cut 1
Add ⅛″
seam
allowance
F

Cut 1
Add ⅛″
seam
allowance

C

Add ⅛″
seam
allowance

Flowering
Wisteria
N   Cut 1

M
Cut 1

Add ⅛″ seam allowance

Spinning Tops *see pages 52 to 55*

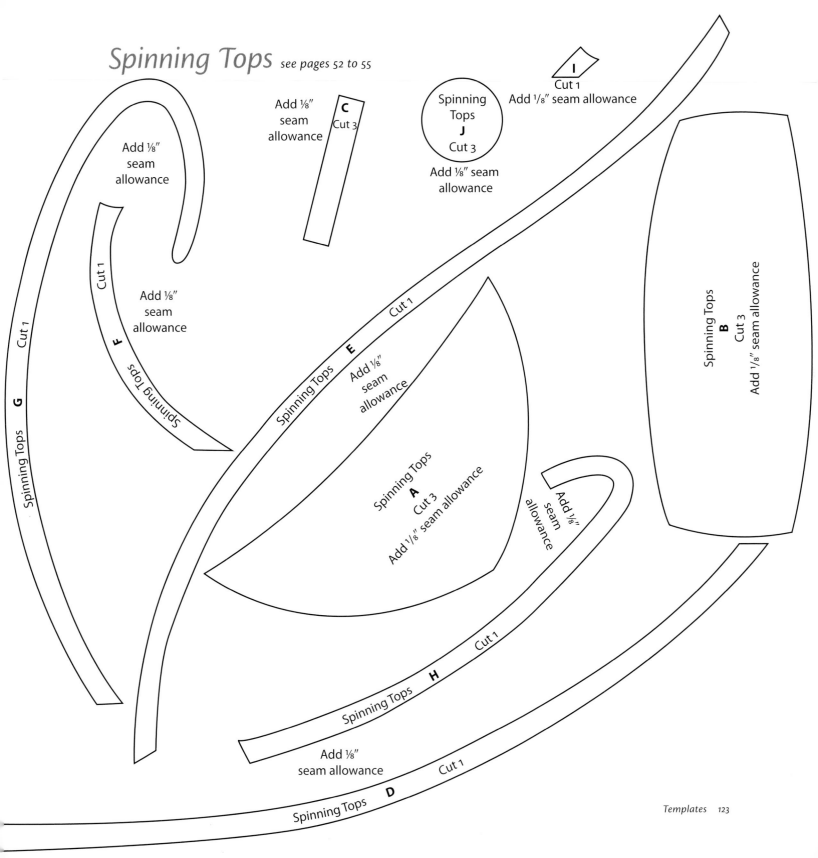

Add ⅛"
seam
allowance

C
Cut 3

Spinning
Tops
J
Cut 3

Add ⅛" seam
allowance

I
Cut 1
Add ⅛" seam allowance

Add ⅛"
seam
allowance

Add ⅛"
seam
allowance

Cut 1

F

Spinning Tops

G

Cut 1

Spinning Tops

Cut 1

Spinning Tops

E

Add ⅛"
seam
allowance

Spinning Tops
A
Cut 3
Add ⅛" seam allowance

Add ⅛"
seam
allowance

Spinning Tops
B
Cut 3
Add ⅛" seam allowance

Cut 1

H

Spinning Tops

Add ⅛"
seam allowance

Cut 1

D

Spinning Tops

Gengi-Ko *see pages 58 to 61*

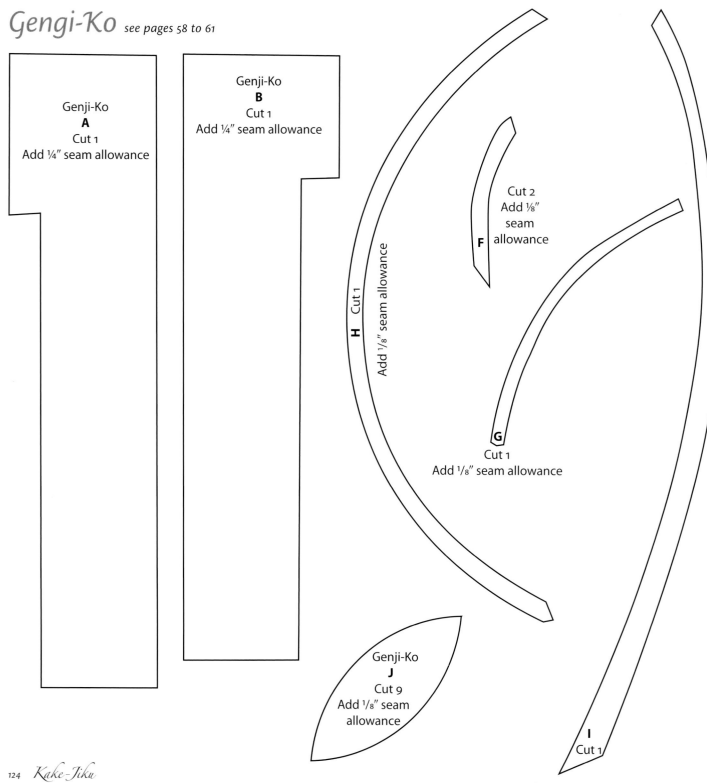

Genji-Ko
A
Cut 1
Add ¼″ seam allowance

Genji-Ko
B
Cut 1
Add ¼″ seam allowance

Cut 2
Add ⅛″
seam
F allowance

H Cut 1
Add ⅛″ seam allowance

G
Cut 1
Add ⅛″ seam allowance

Genji-Ko
J
Cut 9
Add ⅛″ seam
allowance

I
Cut 1

Add ⅛″ seam allowance

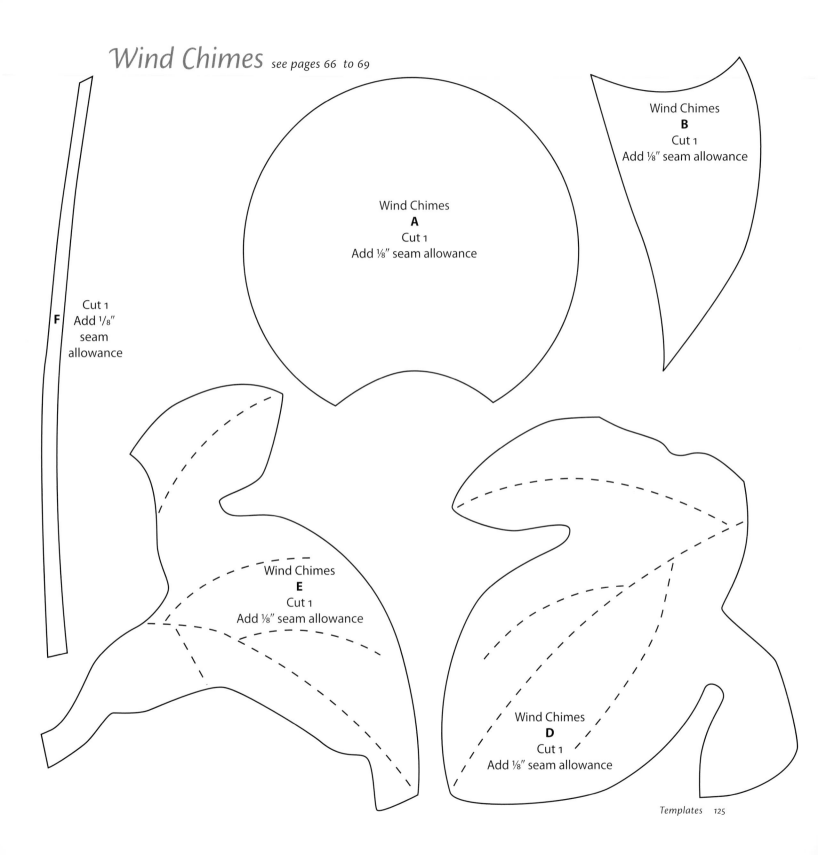

Wind Chimes see pages 66 to 69

Wind Chimes
A
Cut 1
Add ⅛″ seam allowance

Wind Chimes
B
Cut 1
Add ⅛″ seam allowance

F Cut 1
Add ⅛″
seam
allowance

Wind Chimes
E
Cut 1
Add ⅛″ seam allowance

Wind Chimes
D
Cut 1
Add ⅛″ seam allowance

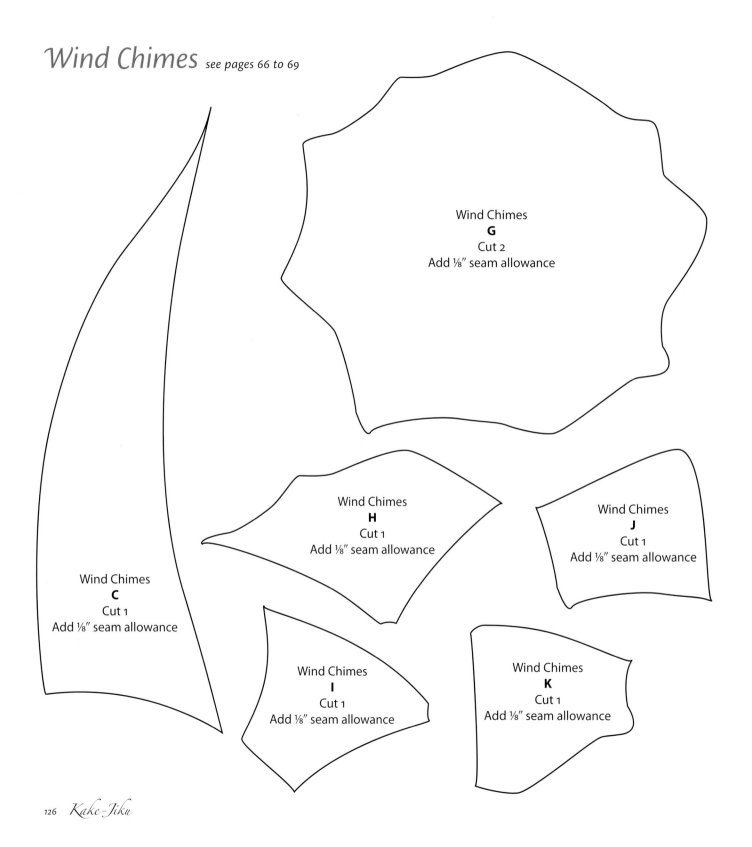

Wind Chimes *see pages 66 to 69*

Wind Chimes
G
Cut 2
Add ⅛" seam allowance

Wind Chimes
H
Cut 1
Add ⅛" seam allowance

Wind Chimes
J
Cut 1
Add ⅛" seam allowance

Wind Chimes
C
Cut 1
Add ⅛" seam allowance

Wind Chimes
I
Cut 1
Add ⅛" seam allowance

Wind Chimes
K
Cut 1
Add ⅛" seam allowance

Wind Chimes see pages 66 to 69

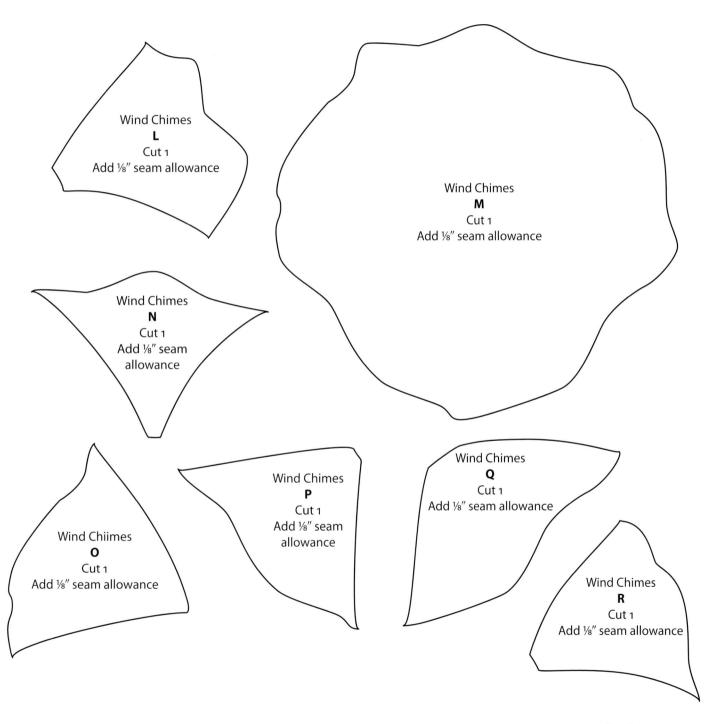

Wind Chimes
L
Cut 1
Add ⅛″ seam allowance

Wind Chimes
M
Cut 1
Add ⅛″ seam allowance

Wind Chimes
N
Cut 1
Add ⅛″ seam
allowance

Wind Chiimes
O
Cut 1
Add ⅛″ seam allowance

Wind Chimes
P
Cut 1
Add ⅛″ seam
allowance

Wind Chimes
Q
Cut 1
Add ⅛″ seam allowance

Wind Chimes
R
Cut 1
Add ⅛″ seam allowance

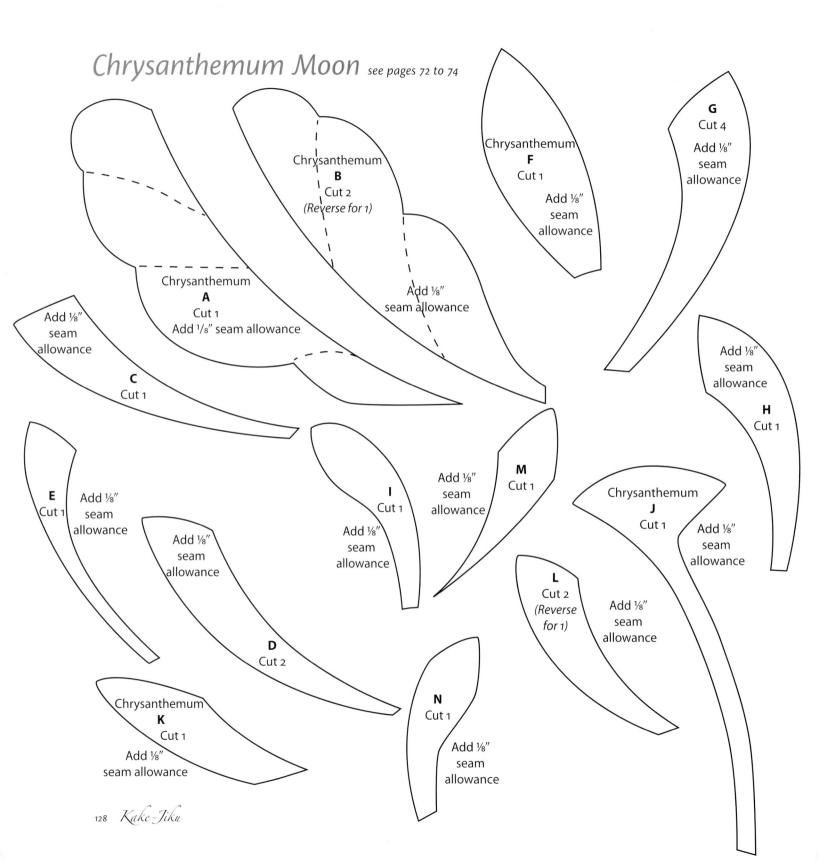

Chrysanthemum Moon *see pages 72 to 74*

Chrysanthemum
A
Cut 1
Add ⅛″ seam allowance

Chrysanthemum
B
Cut 2
(Reverse for 1)

Add ⅛″
seam allowance

Chrysanthemum
F
Cut 1

Add ⅛″
seam
allowance

G
Cut 4

Add ⅛″
seam
allowance

Add ⅛″
seam
allowance

C
Cut 1

Add ⅛″
seam
allowance

H
Cut 1

E
Cut 1

Add ⅛″
seam
allowance

Add ⅛″
seam
allowance

I
Cut 1

Add ⅛″
seam
allowance

Add ⅛″
seam
allowance

M
Cut 1

Add ⅛″
seam
allowance

Chrysanthemum
J
Cut 1

Add ⅛″
seam
allowance

D
Cut 2

L
Cut 2
(Reverse for 1)

Add ⅛″
seam
allowance

Chrysanthemum
K
Cut 1

Add ⅛″
seam allowance

N
Cut 1

Add ⅛″
seam
allowance

Bamboo Blind *see pages 80 to 83*

Bamboo Blind
A
Cut 1
Add ¼" seam allowance

Attach here before cutting fabric

Bamboo Blind *see pages 80 to 83*

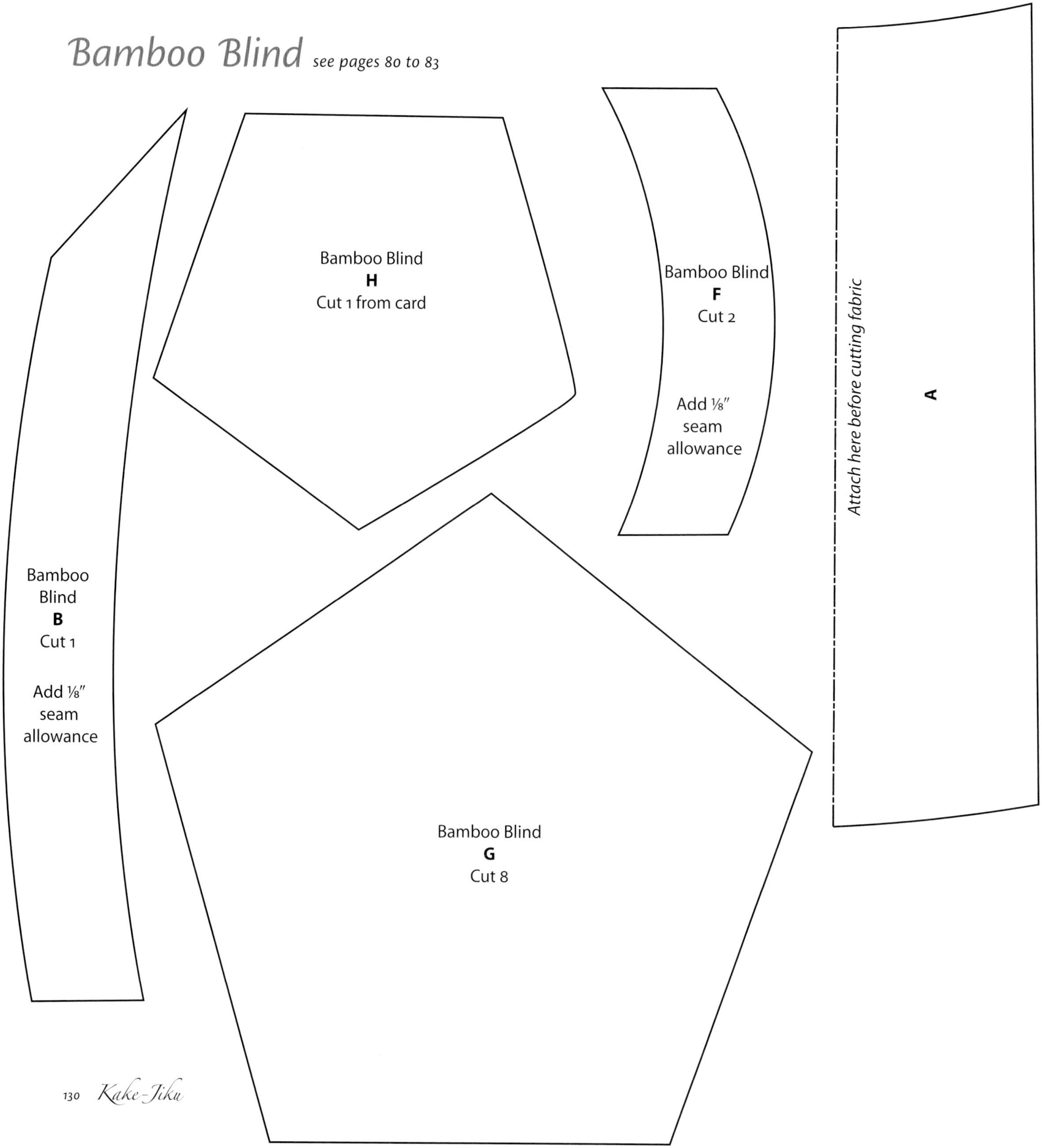

Bamboo Blind
H
Cut 1 from card

Bamboo Blind
F
Cut 2

Add ⅛″
seam
allowance

Bamboo
Blind
B
Cut 1

Add ⅛″
seam
allowance

Bamboo Blind
G
Cut 8

A

Attach here before cutting fabric

Bamboo Blind *see pages 80 to 83*

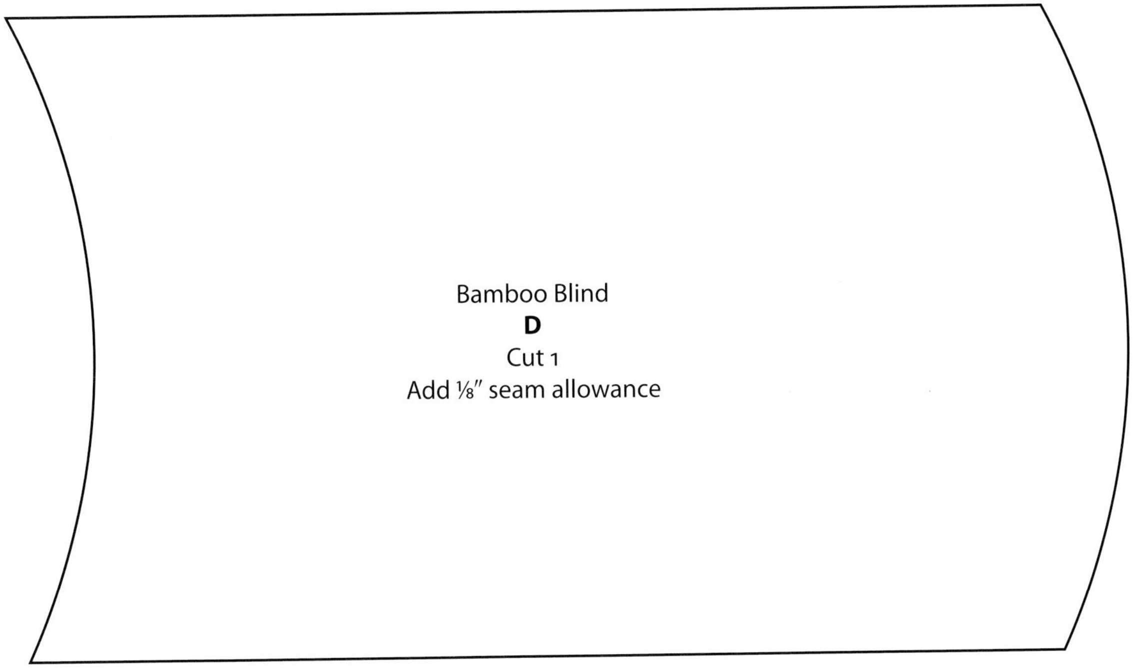

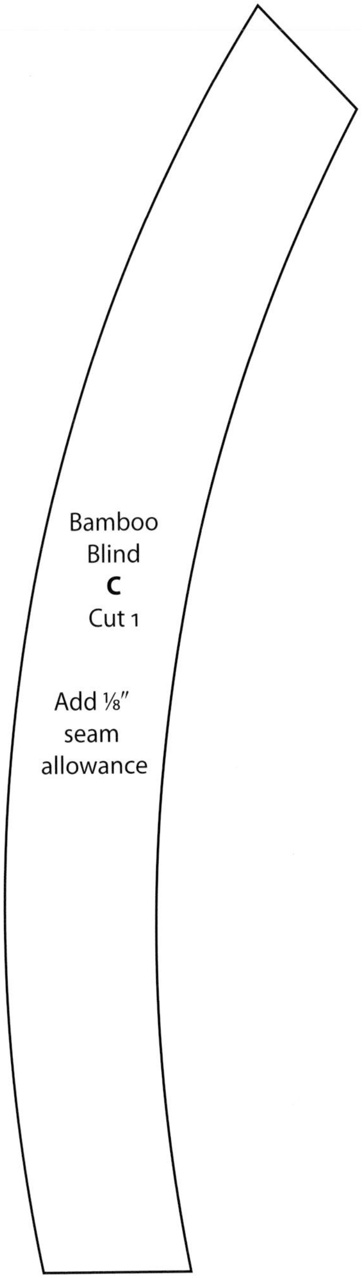

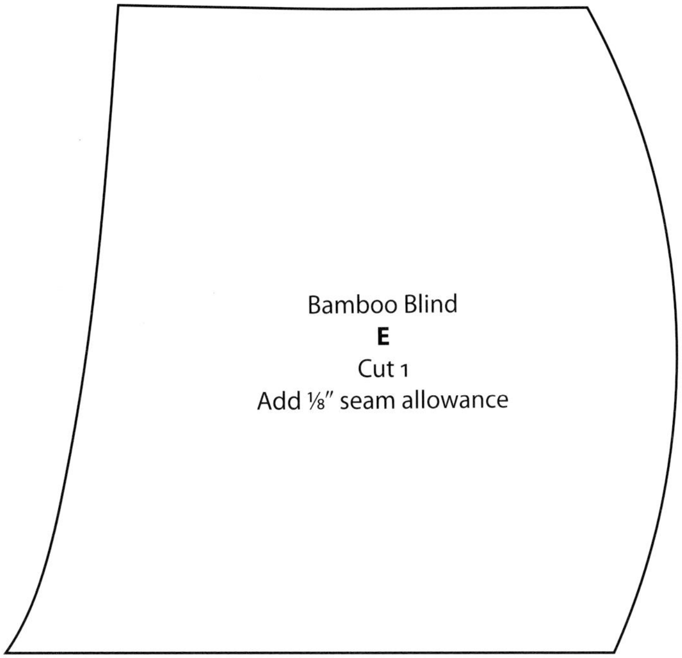

Bamboo Blind
D
Cut 1
Add ⅛" seam allowance

Bamboo
Blind
C
Cut 1

Add ⅛"
seam
allowance

Bamboo Blind
E
Cut 1
Add ⅛" seam allowance

Paper Lantern *see pages 86 to 89*

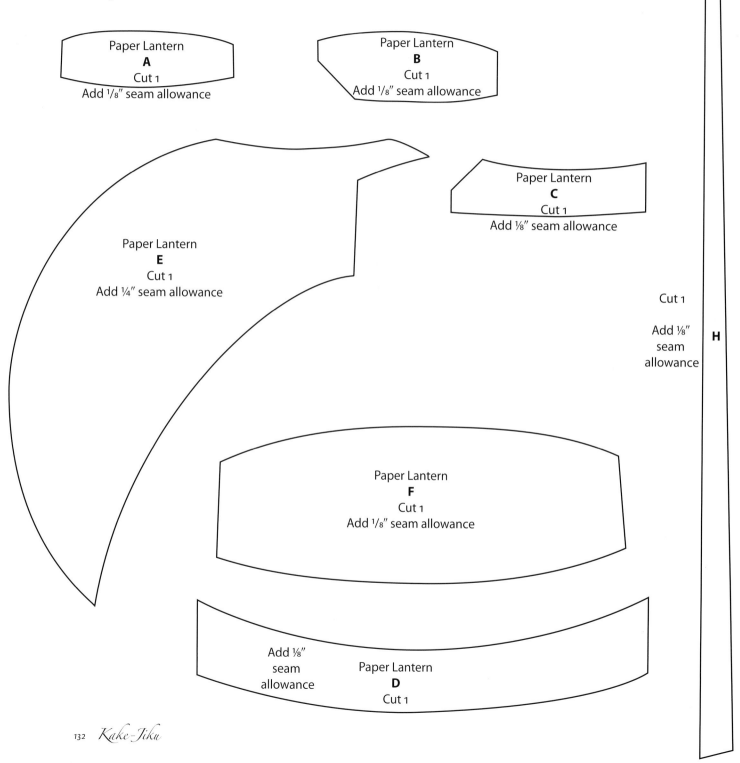

Paper Lantern
A
Cut 1
Add ⅛″ seam allowance

Paper Lantern
B
Cut 1
Add ⅛″ seam allowance

Paper Lantern
C
Cut 1
Add ⅛″ seam allowance

Paper Lantern
E
Cut 1
Add ¼″ seam allowance

Cut 1

Add ⅛″
seam
allowance

H

Paper Lantern
F
Cut 1
Add ⅛″ seam allowance

Add ⅛″
seam
allowance

Paper Lantern
D
Cut 1

Paper Lantern

see pages 86 to 89

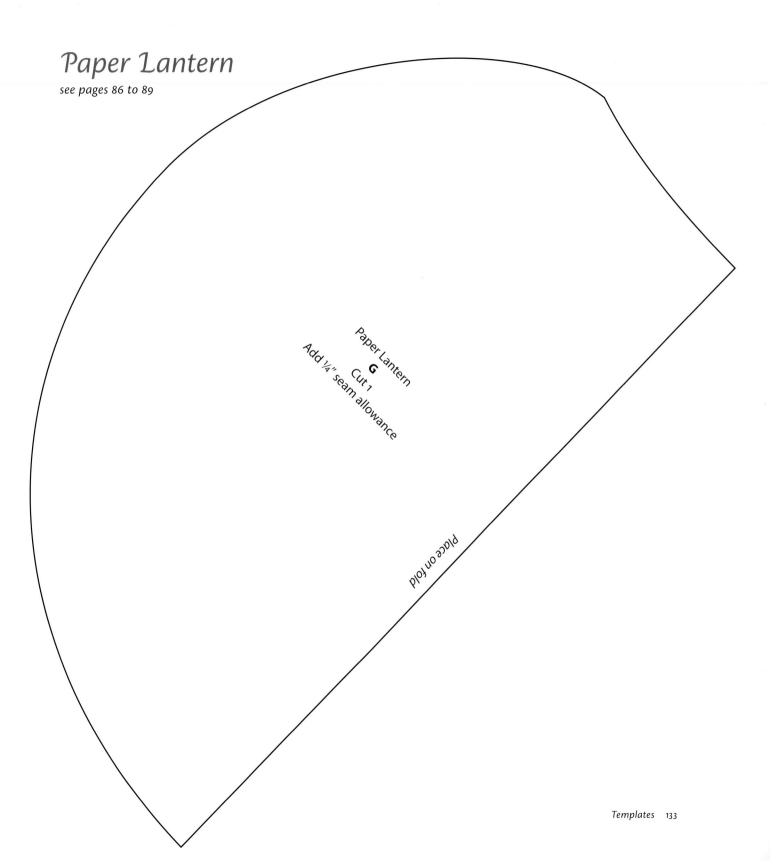

Paper Lantern
G
Cut 1
Add ¼" seam allowance

Place on fold

Reading Under the Vines *see pages 94 to 101*

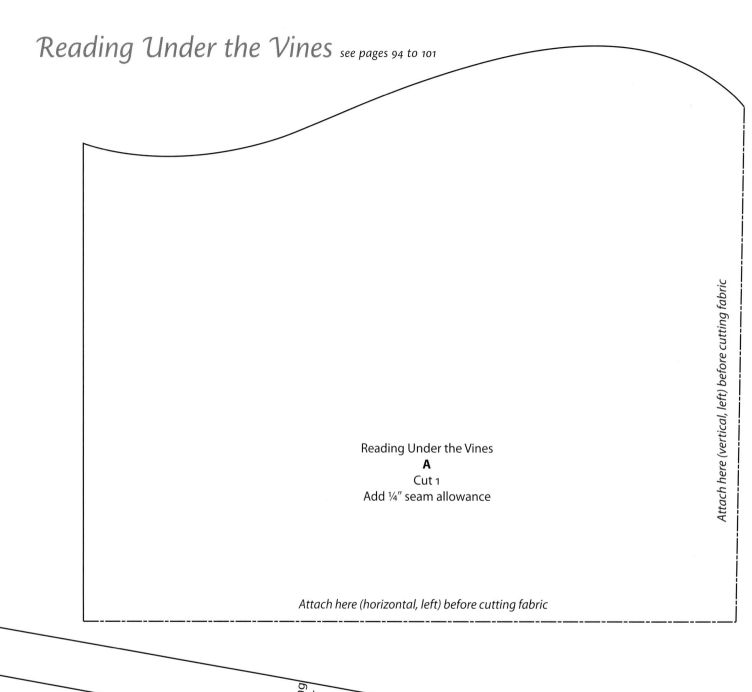

Reading Under the Vines
A
Cut 1
Add ¼" seam allowance

Attach here (vertical, left) before cutting fabric

Attach here (horizontal, left) before cutting fabric

Reading Under the Vines **C** Cut 1

Add ⅛" seam allowance

Reading Under the Vines *see pages 94 to 101*

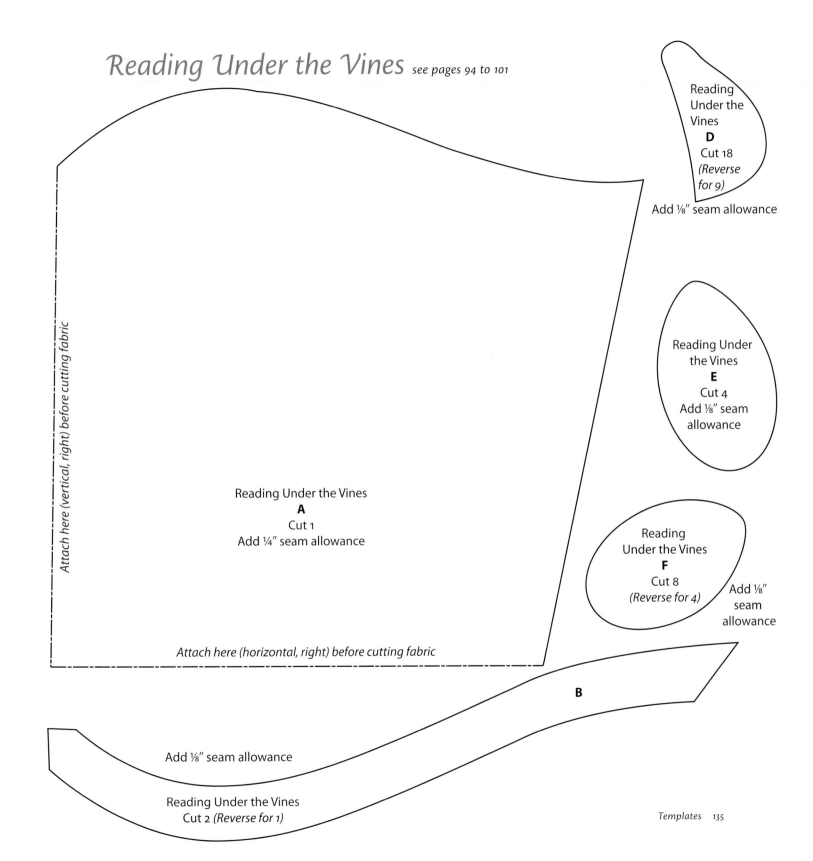

Reading
Under the
Vines
D
Cut 18
(Reverse for 9)

Add ⅛" seam allowance

Reading Under
the Vines
E
Cut 4
Add ⅛" seam
allowance

Reading
Under the Vines
F
Cut 8
(Reverse for 4)

Add ⅛"
seam
allowance

Attach here (vertical, right) before cutting fabric

Reading Under the Vines
A
Cut 1
Add ¼" seam allowance

Attach here (horizontal, right) before cutting fabric

B

Add ⅛" seam allowance

Reading Under the Vines
Cut 2 *(Reverse for 1)*

Reading Under the Vines *see pages 94 to 101*

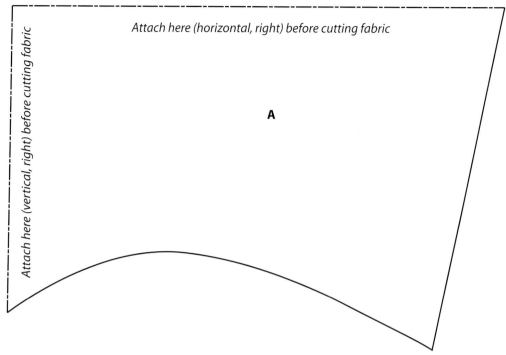

Attach here (horizontal, right) before cutting fabric

Attach here (vertical, right) before cutting fabric

A

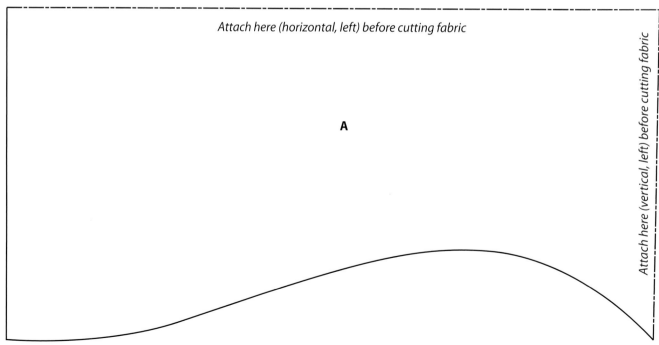

Attach here (horizontal, left) before cutting fabric

Attach here (vertical, left) before cutting fabric

A

Green Tea *see pages 104 to 105*

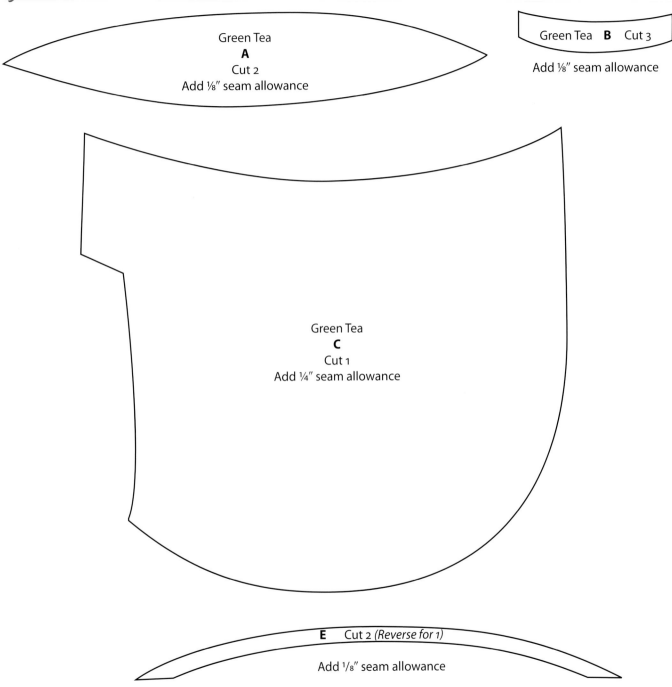

Green Tea
A
Cut 2
Add ⅛″ seam allowance

Green Tea **B** Cut 3

Add ⅛″ seam allowance

Green Tea
C
Cut 1
Add ¼″ seam allowance

E Cut 2 *(Reverse for 1)*

Add ⅛″ seam allowance

Green Tea *see pages 104 to 105*

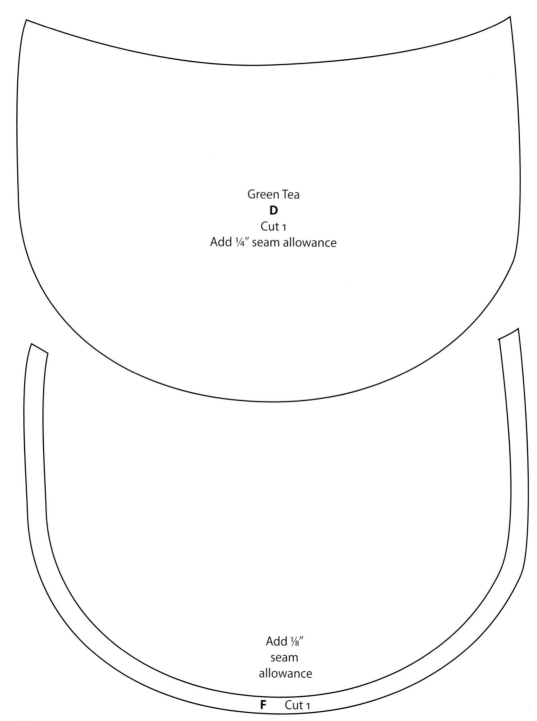

Green Tea
D
Cut 1
Add ¼" seam allowance

Add ⅛"
seam
allowance

F   Cut 1

Crane *see pages 108 to 109*

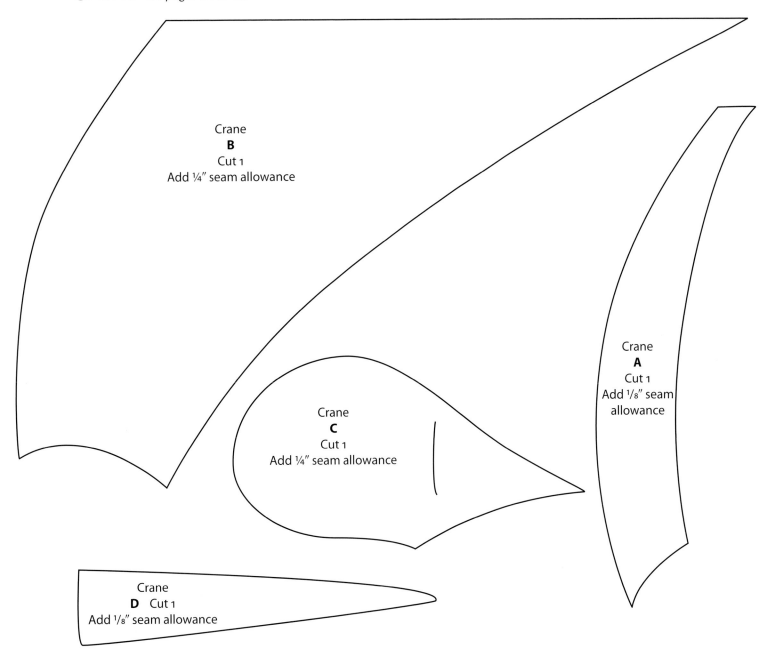

Crane
B
Cut 1
Add ¼″ seam allowance

Crane
A
Cut 1
Add ⅛″ seam allowance

Crane
C
Cut 1
Add ¼″ seam allowance

Crane
D Cut 1
Add ⅛″ seam allowance

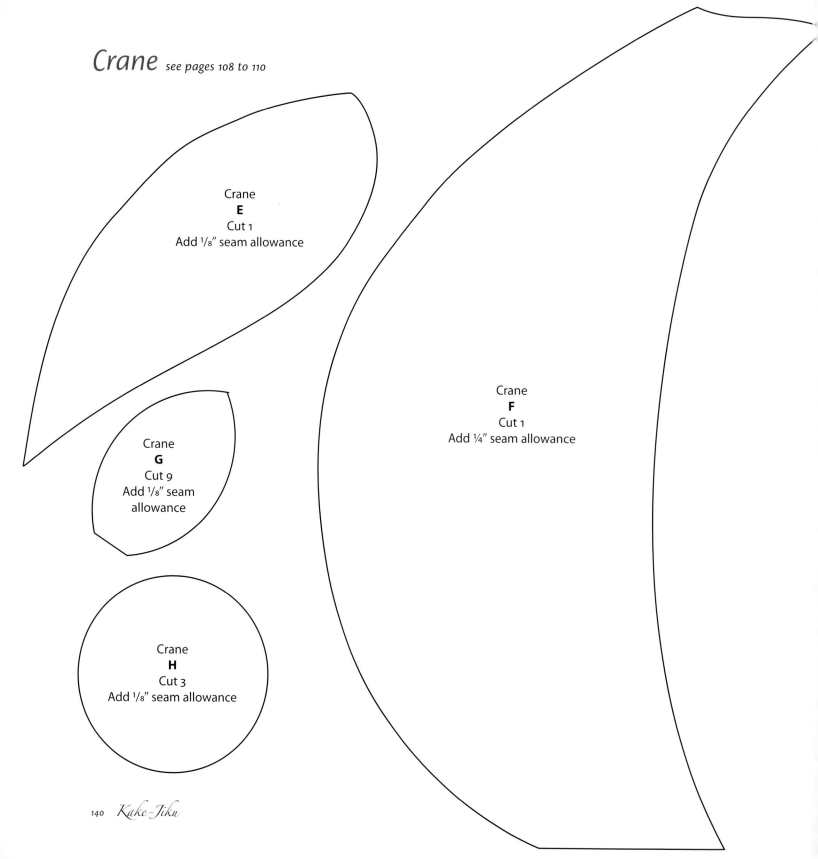

Crane *see pages 108 to 110*

Crane
E
Cut 1
Add ⅛" seam allowance

Crane
F
Cut 1
Add ¼" seam allowance

Crane
G
Cut 9
Add ⅛" seam
allowance

Crane
H
Cut 3
Add ⅛" seam allowance